PLANT PARENTHOOD

Maggie Baylis on Practicing

PLANT PARENTHOOD

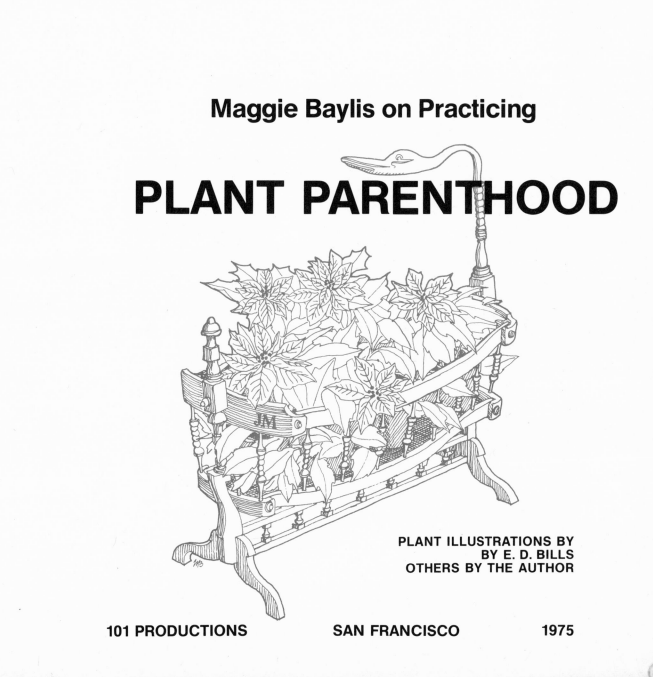

PLANT ILLUSTRATIONS BY
BY E. D. BILLS
OTHERS BY THE AUTHOR

101 PRODUCTIONS   SAN FRANCISCO   1975

TO MY MOTHER
WHOSE PROPAGATION
POTTING & PRUNING
SHAPED MY LIFE

Distributed to the book trade in the United States
by Charles Scribner's Sons, New York, and in Canada
by Van Nostrand Reinhold Ltd., Toronto

Published by 101 Productions
834 Mission Street
San Francisco, California 94103

Library of Congress Cataloging in Publication Data

Baylis, Maggie.
  Maggie Baylis on practicing plant parenthood.

    Includes index.
    1. House plants.   I. Title.   II. Title: Plant
parenthood.
SB419.B26   635.9'65   75-22361
ISBN O-912238-62-3
ISBN O-912238-61-5 pbk.

Contents

Plant Parenthood

"Help! . . . there are too many house plants in the world!" It's a population explosion, a green one! Millions, maybe billions, fill windows in suburbia and ghettos, condominiums and rural schools, on boats and in cook shacks. If rice is the salvation of hungry nations, greens which grow indoors are comforting an emotionally hungry world. From South Africa to Canada, windows have literally turned green.

Increasing confusion and tensions, times when we are rarely in control of anything, least of all our children, the green scene comes through over and over again to reassure us our efforts can bear fruit. After all the bills and headaches and grey mornings, the appearance of a single new shoot on a pot you've nourished and cherished can save a lousy day. A sudden flower stalk appearing on the office *Aloe,* poking up its nose an inch a day, and every one stops by to coo over the baby. This is what makes plant parenthood an on-growing thing. This is what fills those windows: bonuses of hope!

Because we have proved to ourselves we're such neat plant parents, we rush right out again and indiscriminately adopt more and more foster plants—without any real kind of planning about where they go, what they are. And end up with a mess of pottage.

As far as I'm concerned, the only reason to write still another book on house plants is to furnish guidelines to help you develop a new outlook about plants, to discover the unexplored areas of taste and discrimination. Practicing plant parenthood is a much more subtle business than just watering and feeding the plant. It's accepting the responsibility of sharing time and concern. It's choosing the new plant baby very carefully for its background, its relationship to its new siblings, its unique personality.

Like getting a new baby in the family, nothing should ever be the same again for plant parents. Every addition should bring something special: beautiful foliage or bloom which will give added dimension in shadow patterns, something which will refresh your parenthood pleasure each time you stop and look. What I want you to think about is searching out the not usual, not easily found instead of just adding more Boston ferns or Wandering Jews. Instead, indulge in a single big Fluffy Ruffles or Roosevelt fern; look for a Tahitian Bridal Veil, the frothy hanging bouquet which is also a Wanderer.

I want you to discover a new way to look at plants and what they can do to your life style, how to show off their best faces with the addition of drama and theater and moving away from the common. I want you to know it's okay to be a parent to a hundred house plants as it is to two—as long as they don't become just something to water and wean. People who get no playback from plants shouldn't be parents. If your greens are just space fillers, you're littering the world with too much green; the door leads to nowhere. Review your collection: Look with new eyes. Add a back-up plant of great scale; you may see magic.

This book deals earnestly with the responsibility of parenthood. Either give the plant you adopt (or raise in natural childbirth from seeds and cuttings) the conditions and location it likes or don't bring it out of the nursery! Can you lower the thermometer so the room is cooler? Can you adjust light sources so the new pot is pleased? Are you willing to move or remove furniture to make way for a big palm? Will you wash and spray and dunk and pray? Can you keep in mind that you're not a failure if a plant gets sick—or dies? Good gardeners lose plants too and know there's a time to give a plant the heave ho. If you can do these things, you're one neat plant parent!

Clothing the New Baby: Containers

RECONSTITUTED
BABY'S HIGH
CHAIR

I'm all for clay pots: some of my best friends are in them. That's not to discount plastic pots, because they've proved their worth too; they're easier to clean and sterilize (which every pot should experience, incidentally, to remove any spores or bugs left by former tenants). Plastic pots hold water longer, if you have to go away without arranging with a plant sitter. And they are cheaper, too.

But there's something about the organic warmth of a clay pot which strikes a tender note in old planter-uppers. The classic pot is porous, it breathes and it lets out moisture so the roots more quickly absorb the oxygen they need, while the moistened clay sides of the pot cool the soil. The shape allows easy removal of the plant for checking or repotting. Even the drainage hole, protected with its crocking, performs just like the plant doctor ordered. In fact, the pot shape is as near perfect in form and function as the diaper is for the baby.

Plant purists grimly cling to the proposition that a plant in a clay pot should have no distractions. They may be quite right. However, as you may have guessed when you thumb through this book, my ideas of plant parenthood stray from the straight and narrow windowsill row of pots. I believe that the addition of a sculptural container or form, whether serious or lighthearted, ceramic or wood or basket, gives any plant a dimension it can't have otherwise. For example, the two containers on the cover are old friends, but every time a new plant is put in either one of them, I experience a whole new pleasure. An *Episcia* cascading over a face becomes poetic; a *Beaucarnea* is a wild explosion of hair on the little tree trunk. It's simply a matter of lifting out one four-inch pot and inserting another to change moods.

This book is written on the premise that everything changes (even diapers have changed!) and some of these changes include using plants in fresh visual ways to give them more importance. Toss around the idea of being innovative when you clothe a new plant. Changing a baby can turn over a new leaf for Plant Parenthood.

(3" - 5" - 7" AVAILABLE BUT NOT EASILY); REPOT IN NEXT LARGER SIZE: NEVER PUT A SMALL PLANT IN A BIG POT!

PLASTIC LINERS

15" 12" 10" 8" 6" 3" - 4" 2"

CLAY POTS

1-1/2" - 2"

PLASTIC POTS

DOUBLE-POTTING IF SPACE IS LARGE FILL WITH MOISTENED SPHAGNUM FOR PLANTS WHICH NEED HUMIDITY.

GRAVEL OR BLOCK UNDER SMALLER POT SO BOTTOM DOES NOT SIT IN DRAIN WATER.

WOOD TUB

DRILL DRAINAGE HOLES

BUILD A PLYWOOD TRAY WITH 3/8" x 1-3/8" EDGES; LINE WITH FIBERGLASS LIKE A BOAT, TO WATERPROOF.

9

REST A NURSERY CONTAINER ON BRICKS TO RAISE IT IN AN OVERSIZE JAR OR BASKET UNTIL IT IS READY TO BE PERMANENTLY POTTED.

LIFT POT OFF FLOOR TO PREVENT CONDENSA-TION OR DAMAGE TO FLOOR.

1" x 1" STRIPS GLUED TOGETHER

3/8" x 1-3/8" MOLDING TO MAKE A 12" SQ. TRIVET

HALF BARREL

IF INSIDE IS NOT TREATED APPLY CUPRINOL WOOD PRESERVA-TIVE AS DIRECTED.

SOIL LEVEL 1-1/2" BELOW TOP

USE A LARGE PEBBLE TRAY OR GET A PAN TO CATCH DRAIN.

CONTAINERS

BUILD A PLANTER
WHICH CAN BE USED
AS A SINGLE OR IN
ARRANGEMENTS.

Q *I have been given some old clay pots from a friend's greenhouse. They have thick crusts of a kind of white mold. Is there any way to remove that?*

A This white crust is not mold but an accumulation of fertilizer salts over the years. Soak the empty pots in a wash tray in a solution of a cup of household bleach to two gallons of water for at least eight hours. Scrub with a stiff brush, rinse and neutralize the pots by soaking for another eight hours in a solution of one cup of vinegar and two gallons of water. Wash with soap and water and dry. Any stubborn spots can be removed with a wire brush.

Q *Why do my pots leave bleached circles on the floor? I put saucers under the pots.*

A This is not usually leakage but rather condensation. Air space under the saucer will eliminate the problem. Three equal slices from a wine cork, about a quarter inch thick, will lift almost any saucer size and plant weight.

Q *Clay saucers are so expensive I wondered if there is something else I can use under my pots.*

A Inexpensive painted metal trays (plain dark colors), old glass pie plates. You also can apply Rustoleum metal spray paint to flexible aluminum cake and pie tins which are sold in packages in supermarkets.

Q *What can I do? My clay pots are too wide for my windowsill.*

A Get a one-inch piece of shelving six inches wide and the length of your sill. One wood screw at each end will hold it in place (and if you're renting, you can remove board and fill the screw holes before you leave). Cover the board with contact paper, or make a mosaic tile top if you have the urge. If there's a radiator under the window, attach a wider board to deflect the rising heat.

PLAYFUL EQUIPMENT

Being innovative in ways to display house plants may make you self-conscious in the beginning; most of us are basically afraid of doing anything which will make us look silly. Well, let me reassure you: Plants are such positive design forms that as long as they dominate whatever you use or do, they will give you confidence to continue looking for other possibilities—and to uncover your own creativity.

SWINGING POT
(JAPANESE CERAMIC)

CHILD'S PROJECT: CLAY
SLAB BOX & CONES

LINE A BASKET WITH NEWSPAPERS
& A RESIN SEALER
TO WATERPROOF

TWO PLAY-DOUGH BOWLS
SET ONE UPSIDE-DOWN ON
THE OTHER FOR A CRAFT
PROJECT (Recipe: 4 parts
flour, 1 part salt, 1-1/2 parts
water. Mix dry ingredients,
add water & knead. Mold figure;
bake at 300°-325° one hour or
until done. Spray or brush on
clear plastic finish.)

MEXICAN CLAY FISH POT
WITH SUCCULENTS

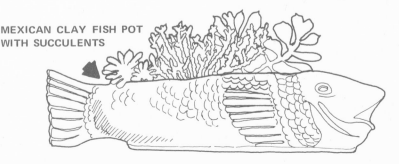

CONTAINERS

WINDOW DISPLAY MANNEQUIN
HEAD AND LEG (check yel-
low pages of telephone directory)

PLAYFUL EQUIPMENT
RECYCLED HANG-UPS

PAPER-WHITE NARCISSUS
PLANTED IN A SHALLOW
PAN WITH PEBBLES &
SET ON A DRAIN TILE
SECTION.

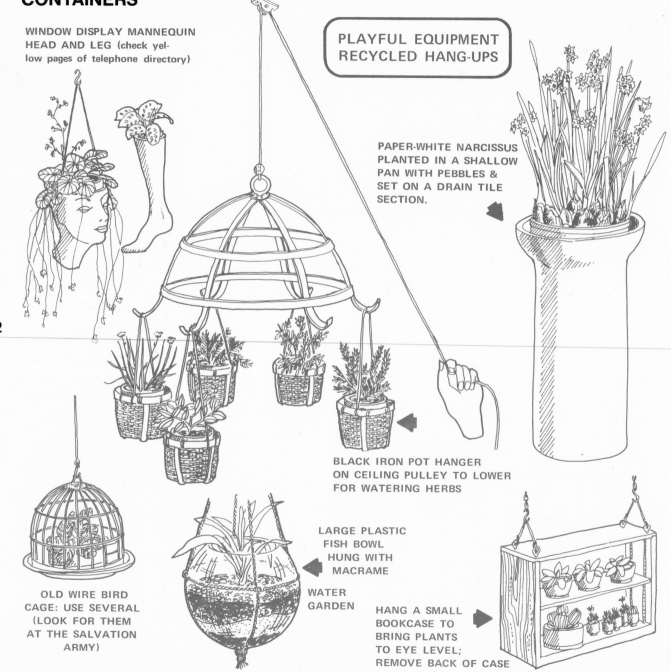

BLACK IRON POT HANGER
ON CEILING PULLEY TO LOWER
FOR WATERING HERBS

OLD WIRE BIRD
CAGE: USE SEVERAL
(LOOK FOR THEM
AT THE SALVATION
ARMY)

LARGE PLASTIC
FISH BOWL
HUNG WITH
MACRAME

WATER
GARDEN

HANG A SMALL
BOOKCASE TO
BRING PLANTS
TO EYE LEVEL;
REMOVE BACK OF CASE

Care and Feeding

POTTING TRAINING

House plants grow in soil. Right? Yes, and they also grow in packaged sterilized mixtures with just the right balance of what good green things need. They grow in soilless mixtures. Some grow in osmunda fibers, firbark or part-sand and part-peat. Some grow on boards with sphagnum moss tied on, like the Staghorn fern. Bromeliads grow on branches. And some plants are grow-in-water babies.

GARDEN SOIL

Soil or loam out of the garden used to be the only material in which to grow or propagate plants. There was nothing else. The *Aspidistra* was potted up, the soil pressed down hard on the roots, and the cast-iron green went on year after year, uncomplaining. That soil would get hard and crusty. No one bothered to change it because there was nothing to replace it that was better.

Soil can be fertile, crumbly and full of good growing elements. But unfortunately such a combination is rare. Most garden soil brought into the house or apartment is high in clay, low in food value and probably populated with nematodes, earthworms, fungi spores and weed seeds. So that you end up with a good potting mixture, it's necessary to sterilize, or pasteurize it. Then you put in the additives.

Pasteurizing soil can be done by baking it in the oven. Once this was a stinking job which drove everyone out of the house. Now by the simple expedient of using a brown-in-bag which is sold in the supermarkets for roasting turkeys, soil is ready for additives after at least an hour in a 180° oven. All you add before baking is a cup of water well mixed through the soil; tie the bag securely and punch one air hole in the top. Place the bag in a roasting pan. When your "mudpie" is done, let it cool completely. Seal the hole with tape and the bag stores the soil, too.

Plants in your garden literally have no limits. Roots can spread, looking for moisture and nourishment. But when you put a pot around six inches of soil, the roots inside will need any good turn they can get.

CARE AND FEEDING: SOIL

SOIL AND DRAINAGE

The most important reason for doctoring garden soil is the drainage factor. Don't worry about fertility or the acid/alkaline content; these can be solved by organic or chemical methods. But drainage has to be right at the start because no matter what you do later, if you've goofed and the water and liquid fertilizers do not drain through the pot, the poor plant is automatically a terminal case.

There are several things to add to be sure drainage is good: sharp builders' sand (don't drag some home from the seashore and expect it to work—it's too high in salt content), peat moss, ground bark, sawdust, leaf mold, and vermiculite or perlite. Optionals are bonemeal and horticultural charcoal. Sand opens up the soil naturally but contributes nothing to its other needs. Peat moss, mentioned over and over again in this book, is partially decayed fibers of bog mosses. It has some food value and gives soil additional acid when needed, but primarily is used to hold water. Never mix peat moss in the soil without first being sure it is completely moistened in warm water. The bark gives some roughage for the little rootlets to wander around and encourages healthier root action; sawdust does this to a lesser degree. Leaf mold is leaves which have dried and decayed; they furnish the organic matter so essential to the richness of soil.

There are two opposing camps on when to use vermiculite, when to use perlite. Actually, they both perform a similar function: They are porous and insure excellent aeration of the soil. Vermiculite is a mineral which can hold up to 10 times its weight in water. Perlite is a volcanic porous rock, but some dislike its insistent white look in the dark soil. Perlite is often used in place of coarse sharp sand. Vermiculite acts like a sponge yet never gets soggy. It is available in bags; again, check labels to be sure you're getting horticultural grade. Both provide dry storage for resting bulbs.

PACKAGED SOIL

There is no single soil which will do everything for every plant. Packaged soils are a great addition for indoor gardeners; they are sterilized and free of noxious baddies. But no two plants are alike and some want more, just like children who are never satisfied. If anything negative can be said about the packaged mixture, it is that it's a finer mixture than natural soil. By adding moistened peat moss you will increase the roughage. Leaf mold will do a similar job. Keep in mind that some plants are lime-lovers and will not go for the acid-building peat; check the plant's case history.

When you buy packaged soil, also check the contents of the mixture on the bag. Some will be mostly firbark and chopped leaf mold, others may be mostly peat moss. If you're not sure, ask the store manager to give you a recommendation. Whatever you buy, always moisten the mixture before you put it in the pot. Some manufacturers give firm label instructions to pour water right into the bag and to knead it and let stand until the water is absorbed.

15

USE BOILING WATER
TO MOISTEN SPHAGNUM
MOSS; COOL AND SQUEEZE
OUT EXCESS WATER.

SOILLESS SOIL

The usual content of soilless mixtures is peat, perlite and vermiculite. This produces a lightweight clean mix which holds in moisture and gives an extra boost to blooming house plants not available in ordinary garden soils. You can put together your own formula or buy it in nursery centers. Organic fertilizer is more effective than chemical, which washes out too fast.

To repeat, no one mixture is right for all plants. You will have to experiment and exchange "recipes" with other plant parents. For special growing conditions, such as required for African violets, your best bet is to buy the special soil recommended for these touchy gesneraids. There is also a cactus mix available.

Additional soil additives: Wood shavings add humus to larger house plants. Redwood sawdust is high in acid reaction, and if your water is alkaline, it will help the battle for survival; used as a mulch, it cuts the speed of evaporation from the surface. If sawdust is used, it creates a nitrogen "draft" on the soil, and added bonemeal is called for. Ground coconut husks and gravel are sometimes added to orchid mix but give no additional nourishment.

Science continually comes up with something new. Now it is a product called Hydrogel, a water-retention material made by Union Carbide. Tests indicate it can be mixed with soil; good growth is indicated with one-sixth to one-eighth the usual frequency of watering. Add an ounce and a half of Hydrogel to a three-pound coffee can of soil mix (two parts peat, one part sand, one part perlite).

HUMUS

Q *Where can I get humus to mix into the soil?*

A Humus is decomposed or decayed organic matter, like green leafy vegetables, peat or compost residue. The last is an ideal source of humus—everyone should be familiar with a compost pile.

OSMUNDA

Q *I was told to plant my tree orchids in osmunda fiber; what is that?*

A This material is the roots of the osmunda or Cinnamon fern. It is also used in planting some bromeliads and other orchids.

LIMESTONE

Q *You mention limestone being added in small quantities for some plants. Where do I get it?*

A Powdered limestone is available in small packages at nurseries. This is for house plants which do not like acid. Ask for horticultural limestone. You can make your own version by grinding eggshells in a mortar bowl or in the blender. The limestone you buy will assimilate faster, is less messy.

PEAT MOSS

Q *Is peat moss the same thing as sphagnum moss?*

A Peat moss is decomposed sphagnum bog moss. It has to be shredded to mix well with other additives. Sphagnum is a coarse dried material which is used as a mulch on top of soil in pots and in between pots when one double-pots a plant. It seems to resist fungus, which is a bonus considering that it can take in about 20 times its weight in water.

LOAM

Q *Is there any difference between soil and loam?*

A The average loam has about half silt, one-fourth clay and one-fourth sand. Loam is soil which holds nutrients and water. Most soil is imbalanced in one or more of these components.

17

LEAF MOLD

Q *When I put leaf mold into soil, what should be its consistency?*

A The leaves should be decayed to the point that they are flaky, but not just dust.

PROVEN SOIL MIXTURES

To make a general house plant mixture:
2 parts garden soil, pasteurized
1 part leaf mold
1 part sharp sand
1 teaspoon bonemeal to each five gallons of mix

To make a soilless mixture:
1 part peat moss
1 part perlite
1 part vermiculite

To make a mixture for succulents and cacti:
1 part peat moss
2 parts perlite
2 parts coarse sand or vermiculite

CARE AND FEEDING: POTTING

1 CLEAN POT

CROCKING

DRAIN HOLE

POT-LUCK IS JUST DOING WHAT THE EXPERTS DO NATURALLY

2 SOIL MIXTURE

PEAT MOSS

SMALL ROCKS OR GRAVEL

LARGER, OLDER PLANTS MAY NOT LET GO OF THE POT. USE A LONG KNIFE BLADE TO RUN AROUND THE EDGE & RELEASE STUBBORN ROOTS.

ALWAYS* MOISTEN THE SOIL FIRST SO IT STICKS TOGETHER & THE PLANT DOESN'T LEAVE THE POT WITH BARE BOTTOM SHOWING.

3 REMOVE A PLANT BY KNOCKING IT OUT ON THE EDGE OF COUNTER.

HOLD A HAND OVER SOIL AND POT TO HAVE A FIRM GRIP WHEN IT LETS GO.

4 IF ROOTS ARE SPONGY OR UNHEALTHY, CUT THEM OFF WITH SHARP SHEARS.

IF ROOTS ARE BADLY POT BOUND, LOOSEN THEM WITH THE TINES OF A FORK.

IF OLD CROCKING IS SMOTHERED BY ROOTS, LOOSEN IT.

5 IF THE PLANT HAS MORE THAN ONE STEM IT CAN BE DIVIDED; TRY FIRST TO PULL IT APART. SOME MUST BE CUT APART: SHAKE SOIL OFF ROOTS, THEN CUT THROUGH PLANT'S CROWN WITH A STERILE KNIFE. REPOT AS FAST AS POSSIBLE.

6 Water newly potted plant thoroughly & keep out of sun. Allow 2 weeks to take hold.
*Do not water a succulent or cactus before repotting. Wait a week to water after.

PUTTING THE HOUSE PLANT TO BED: POTTING

Of *course* everyone knows how to pot a plant. Not true. Plants are unpredictable; they play games with you just like small children do the first time you have to put them to bed. Unless you start with a sure, firm hand and let them know *you* know what you're doing, the bedtime story has an unhappy ending.

I find that really good gardeners, outdoor gardeners, are sometimes at a loss about the way to put a house plant in a pot. They're adept at knocking young bedding seedlings out of plastic containers and transplanting to the vegetable row. But to manage a soft-vining *Clerodendrum* with all its tentacles going every which way, into a new pot, takes a special knack. So, even though you may be an old hand, you can refresh yourself on the repetition of potting techniques for the next few minutes. Or, you can skip one space and go directly to Propagating.

Various kinds of pots were dealt with in the container section, in case you're a skip-around reader. You have the pot and you're ready to go: First step is a *clean* pot. If it is new, you can go right ahead and plant. However, the cost of pots has gone out of reach and we all scrounge around hoping to find old ones which will do. That means giving the used pot, if it is clay, a vigorous wire-brushing to remove stains or white marks. Then for any kind of used container, a soapy scrubbing and dunking in a mild solution of household bleach removes the leftover soil, cobwebs and any fungi spores which may be hiding in the pores. No matter how many times you insist on this cleanup, impatient people will grab any pot at hand and start filling, only to find the otherwise healthy plant on its way to an unhappy ending.

CARE AND FEEDING: POTTING

TAKING POT LUCK NEEDS PLANNING

Finding a place to work, a place to keep the few tools you need, storage for plant food, the mister, and a washable surface gets complicated if you live in an apartment or a mobile home or a retirement condominium. Any place near water—the sink, the tub with a board stretched across, the top of the washing machine—will do. A painter's drop cloth made of plastic will protect the flat area and can be used over and over.

Organize your soil, the pot, the plant. A big mixing bowl is an answer for moistening packaged soil. Crock the pot and add a layer of moistened peat moss or crushed *un*salted peanut shells over a thin layer of gravel; put some of the soil on top and next comes the plant. Some plants, particularly large ones, must not have their root ball damaged or broken and are transferred to the new container and set on the new soil. Additional soil is dribbled around the edges and firmed with a long flat stick as you add each additional bit of soil. Small or young plants, the tender variety, can have their roots spread over the first layer and more soil carefully added so it covers all the roots. While you are doing this, hold the plant's main stem so it doesn't bend. Give the pot a light bouncing on the work surface to settle the soil. The finished job should leave the plant's relationship to the soil the same as it was in its original container. *Don't* fill any pot right to the top—always leave at least half an inch to one inch for watering space.

Read the description of the plant and check its watering needs after repotting. If water required, do so slowly, carefully, so nothing is disturbed. Drain away the excess and stand the newly planted one on a saucer to protect. Keep away from sunlight for a few days. Don't add additional water, unless the plant looks wilty; then only mist leaves.

SUNNY-DISPOSITION PLANTS

PLASTIC OR METAL CAN

1
Bring your new plant home from the nursery & leave it outdoors for two weeks; keep leaves misted. Let it get used to you . . .

2
Borrow a can cutter or tin snips to cut open container. Be careful you don't break root ball. Pot up in its new container. Insure drainage with good soil mixture & crocking.

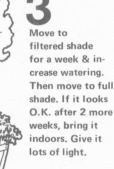

3
Move to filtered shade for a week & increase watering. Then move to full shade. If it looks O.K. after 2 more weeks, bring it indoors. Give it lots of light.

SHY-IN-THE-SHADE PLANTS: Move indoors from the nursery with few problems.

SPRING PLANTING: TEACHING A LARGE OUTDOOR PLANT TO COME IN WITHOUT STRAIN

SHOPPING: Depend on a top-notch nursery. Shop in spring when new leaves are busting out all over.

SELECT the best shape for its new space indoors. Roots poking out of container? Plant is root bound, a handicap for the already stressed new conditions. A plant which has been living outdoors all its life needs every plus it can get.

WASH OFF the foliage with a hose when it arrives from the nursery. Give it a hefty drink to leach out any accumulated fertilizer salts, then hold back water to a minimum.

PRUNE out broken tips. Pinch back new growth. Check for signs of disease.

21

CARE & FEEDING: Feed only half the amount labels recommend, twice as often to avoid root burn. Don't fertilize in winter.

Leaf drop is normal: If foliage droops & leaves curl under, raise the moisture in the air; it's too hot, too dry. Set the container on a moist pebble tray. Each year, give a housebroken plant an outing to deck or patio, in shade.

CARE AND FEEDING: POTTING

DIRTY POTS

Q *Why all this fussing about a little dirt on a pot?*

A Put a plant in a pot which hasn't been sterilized and you expose it to all the dangers which beset the plant before it. Fungus which caused crown rot will still be around to work on the successor. Spider mites have a nasty way of keeping in touch with anything new and succulent.

DRAINAGE

Q *If the special soil mixture gives good drainage, why do I have to bother with putting that piece of broken pot over the drainage hole?*

A That broken bit of pot is called "crocking," and it allows the water to drain under and out without being blocked by roots. The curved outside of the broken shard should be up so there is a space under. If you put a plant in a pot without this important step, the plant may grow without problems; but it could develop root rot if there's a blockage. Repot a new plant right away if it has no crocking.

Q *I would like to plant in a pot which has no drainage hole. Is this possible?*

A For some plants, but you will have to learn to be a conscientious waterer. Because the water has no place to go except into the plant's system, it must be given in small doses, perhaps more often. Fill the bottom of the container at least an inch deep with small stones, small pieces of broken pots. Then a quarter-inch layer of gardeners' charcoal and the soil and you are ready to plant. If the pot is bigger than six inches, make the stone or gravel layer up to two inches deep. Depending on the texture of the container, it is possible to drill a hole in the bottom with an electric hand drill and a silicon-carbide tipped bit. Earthenware and plastic can be treated this way.

HEAVY POTS

Q *I have a big Fiddle Leaf fig, but it's too heavy for me to repot alone. What should I do?*

A You can have it repotted by a local nursery—which is the expensive answer. Or, you can "top-dress" it by scraping away as much of the soil around the plant as you can without disturbing the roots and add new soil. As well as helping the fig, it will make it look fresh and neat. If you can find someone with strong arms willing to help, the fig can be removed from the pot and set on newspapers; by rubbing away as much soil around the roots as possible and putting the fig back in the same tub with new soil tamped around the edges, you've really "repotted."

ORCHID SOIL

Q *When I repot my orchid, should I look for a different kind of soil?*

A In repotting any plant keep the mixture you add as nearly like the original as possible. Switching puts stresses on which are unnecessary.

POT SIZES

Q *I planted the Coffee tree someone gave me in a large pot right away because I thought it would grow faster. It died.*

A My sympathy goes out to you, Jim. Next time remember that you never put a plant in a pot with a diameter two inches greater than the original pot. If there is too much new soil around the edge of the pot, the moisture and food goes down without ever getting to the small root ball in the center.

REPOTTING

Q *How will I know when to repot?*

A There are several obvious signs: Plants which show signs of looking wilty a couple of hours after you water—the moisture may not be getting through the root mass. Are the lower leaves looking yellowish, sickly? The nourishment is going to the newer leaves. Also, when the leaf size gets smaller and smaller, the plant may be calling for help. Some plants can stay in the same containers for years. Check the plant details which appear later for more information.

WOOD TUBS

Q *The soy tubs I planted two years ago are rotting at the bottom. How should I avoid this if I replant in the same kind again?*

A Treating the wood with copper naphthanate helps to prevent decay. Don't use creosote or other outdoor preservatives. Lifting the pot up on cleats so air circulates is a good idea.

ESPALIERED FRUIT TREE

PLANTER IS EASY-TO-BUILD 1″ x 12″ ROUGH REDWOOD, STAINED; BAMBOO STAKES PAINTED BLACK.

WATER GARDENING: THE AGE OF AQUARIUMS

Bringing up house plants which take to water has become a "cool" item. It's not a new idea, but the way it all goes together brings new visual delight. There are at least two dozen familiar indoor greens who got their start in the dim past in moister conditions than most plants. The bog plants, or sedges like *Cyperus* and *papyrus,* are natural water-babies; Chinese Evergreen, *Coleus,* ivy, Screw pine, Wandering Jew, Moses-in-a-Boat can grow either way because they insist on the extra water their systems need, in soil.

With the advent of water gardening, webfoot greens move out of soil beds and into waterbeds—and they love it! The exciting part is that these aquatics look so great through the clear glass of an aquarium-type container. Plastic and glass in classic pot shapes are acceptable as water garden jars. However, I feel that this newly popular way of planting deserves something special in a container, something with more imagination. Suggestions are sketched on the next two pages.

Suggestions are sketched on the next two pages.

Decide whether you want several plants of one kind or one each of several kinds. A distinctive bowl like a glass soufflé dish planted with four or five Chinese Evergreen taken from four-inch pots will become a stunning centerpiece in six months, crowned with those lovely calla-like pale cream blossoms.

Starting with plants bought from a nursery is the simplest way to sure of what you're getting. It is possible to plant water-rooted cuttings you start yourself, but soil-grown cuttings take hold faster. Water-induced roots develop differently, and when they're taken out of the water and potted they are not prepared to extract oxygen in the same way from soil. The resulting plant is slow-growing. Even though the plant becomes a water-garden tenant, it will have its feet in vermiculite and sand, and this condition is like planting in soil.

Other water-babies: *Dieffenbachia, Pleomele, Philodendron,* Spathe flower, *Acorus,* croton, Ti, *Dracaena,* Swedish ivy.

CUT OFF TOP OF
JUG & PLANT
CROTON OR DRACAENA

WATER-BABIES
PLANTS WHICH GROW
SWIMMINGLY IN WATER
AS WELL AS IN SOIL

25

COLEUS IN
JELLY GLASSES

JAPANESE
SWEET FLAG
IN WINE
CARAFE

MOSES-IN-A-BOAT

CHINESE EVERGREEN; MULTIPLE
PLANTS IN GLASS SOUFFLÉ DISH
OR SALAD BOWL

CREEPING FIG

SMALL LEAF IVY

PLASTIC SWEATER BOX

CARE AND FEEDING: WATER GARDENS

HOW TO START A WATER GARDEN

Start by washing container and tools in soapy water; wash any small stones or gravel to be used. This is insurance against fungus spores which like to play in water, too. Remove plants from pots and wash all dirt off roots.

To plant, put a layer of gravel on the bottom, then a sprinkling of gardeners' charcoal to keep water sweet. Hold the just-washed plant where you'd like it in the container and carefully fill around the roots. You have three choices of material at this point: vermiculite is an excellent growing medium, or you can make the planting all fine gravel, or you can layer colored sand to give a stratified pattern. Add a layer of washed marble chips to dress the top.

Mix a gallon of water and one-fourth the amount of liquid fertilizer recommended on the bottle for that quantity of water. Pour on the garden until it reaches half an inch below the top level. Add once a week from that mixture; drain and replace every six weeks (if you used sand, eliminate this step and just water to keep level even).

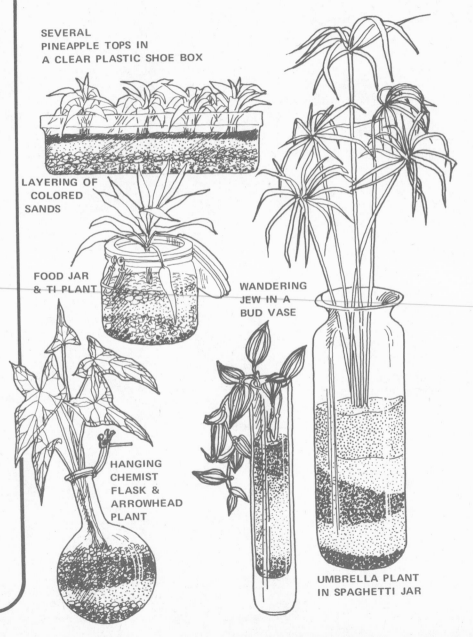

SEVERAL PINEAPPLE TOPS IN A CLEAR PLASTIC SHOE BOX

LAYERING OF COLORED SANDS

FOOD JAR & TI PLANT

WANDERING JEW IN A BUD VASE

HANGING CHEMIST FLASK & ARROWHEAD PLANT

UMBRELLA PLANT IN SPAGHETTI JAR

PROPAGATING: NATURAL PLANT PARENTHOOD

Once you've gained that good feeling about being a neat foster parent to the plants you've adopted, it's time to try raising plants from scratch: cuttings, seeds, leaves, stolons, layering, offsets, bulbs, rhizomes, tubers, spores. Don't let that long list turn you off; the names given to the act of starting plants from those you have rather than buying potted carbon copies, are clues to the miracles of growth in the green world.

Take the cutting: It is the simplest way to get going. When you midwife the birth of a new *Ficus benjamina* from two leaves and stem cut from your favorite fig, you may decide to grow all your plants the natural birth method!

CUTTINGS

Words like "cuttings" are so much a part of gardeners' language one is apt to forget that there are newcomers who have no idea how to "take" a cutting: A "cutting" is the tip of a stem of a branching plant with leaves attached, which can be removed, or taken, with scissors or a sharp knife. With a proper start, this live stick can manufacture its own roots; it can carry on all the processes of the parent plant, and if destined to have flowers, will oblige by doing just that. And in time, it will become a mature shape which can be the parent of more cuttings.

There are several methods to start the roots of a cutting. Different plants respond different ways. But once the cuttings develop healthy root systems, your tender concern has paid off. The two commonest types of cuttings are hardwood stems and soft stems. Hardwood will take longer to root, and should be taken during the growing period, from late spring through summer. Soft stems will root in water, and may be ready for planting in two to three weeks. Spring and summer are best times to try, but soft stems generally can be rooted any time of the year. Keep all cuttings out of direct sunlight.

CARE AND FEEDING: PROPAGATION

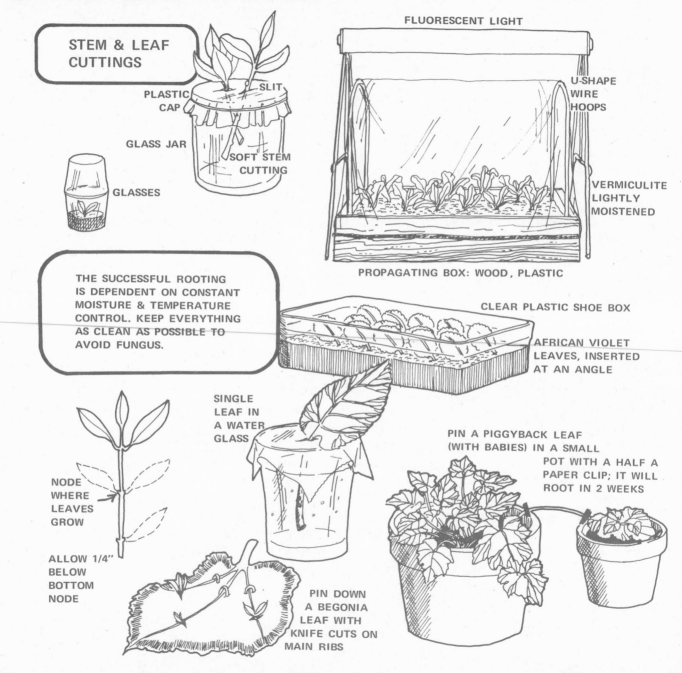

STEM & LEAF CUTTINGS

PLASTIC CAP

SLIT

GLASS JAR

GLASSES

SOFT STEM CUTTING

FLUORESCENT LIGHT

U-SHAPE WIRE HOOPS

VERMICULITE LIGHTLY MOISTENED

PROPAGATING BOX: WOOD, PLASTIC

THE SUCCESSFUL ROOTING IS DEPENDENT ON CONSTANT MOISTURE & TEMPERATURE CONTROL. KEEP EVERYTHING AS CLEAN AS POSSIBLE TO AVOID FUNGUS.

CLEAR PLASTIC SHOE BOX

AFRICAN VIOLET LEAVES, INSERTED AT AN ANGLE

SINGLE LEAF IN A WATER GLASS

PIN A PIGGYBACK LEAF (WITH BABIES) IN A SMALL POT WITH A HALF A PAPER CLIP; IT WILL ROOT IN 2 WEEKS

NODE WHERE LEAVES GROW

ALLOW 1/4" BELOW BOTTOM NODE

PIN DOWN A BEGONIA LEAF WITH KNIFE CUTS ON MAIN RIBS

CUTTINGS

Q *Do I keep all the leaves on the stem I cut?*

A No, remove at least half, leaving two or three at the tip. There should be at least two nodes below leaves where roots can start. Cuttings from small-leaf plants can be from two to eight inches long, depending on the leaf dimension. To support young tender stems, cover the glass of water with a thin plastic scrap held in place with a rubber band; make slits to slip the stems through into the water. Large-leaf cuttings can be almost any length but will take a large glass jar to accommodate water-rooting; when rooting in a propagating box, support vining types.

Q *Is there anything which will make a cutting root more successfully?*

A You can purchase a hormone powder that will give any cutting started in moist-to-touch vermiculite a big boost. Just dip the cutting end in the powder before planting.

Q *Why do some leaves root and others don't?*

A Leaves from plants which don't branch and large fleshy or hairy leaves take to rooting. Thin leaves or hard ones don't and you have to depend on stem cuttings. Begonias and African violets are a cinch to leaf-root, particularly under lights.

Q *I tried potting a cutting but it started to wilt.*

A Some plants suffer from severance from the mother. If you put the pot and plant in a closed plastic bag it should make the move okay. Give it a little air each day, and remove the bag after a week.

Q *How close should cuttings started in a box be to the light?*

29

A Three inches to a foot from fluorescent lights. The box should have a tent of clear plastic and be kept warm, 75° if possible. Check at the end of a week for signs of roots; if they're not ready, stick the cutting back for another wait. Some take up to four weeks for incubation before potting.

THANKSGIVING
CACTUS

CHRISTMAS
CACTUS

EASTER
CACTUS

SEEDS

Growing a plant from a single seed takes all the patience of a parent. It is slow and demands your attention more than propagating by other methods. But it may be the only way you can raise a rare foliage because you may never find the plant in your shopping.

There are seed-growing enthusiasts who delight in the challenge, who are interested in the genetic development. They grow seeds so small a magnifying glass is used to sow them. To me, however, the fun of seeds is starting a Sea Grape, or a Horseradish tree, or a *Cassia,* the tropical shower tree. (Check at the end of this section for Sources of Seeds.) The fascination is being able to start an exotic which lives outdoors in the tropics—and making it a happy house plant.

Basically, two things are essential to seed propagation: moisture and bottom warmth. Covering the seed-growing box or pot with thin clear plastic keeps that moisture in the potting material. Bottom warmth can be solved by putting the container on top of a water heater (keep it away from any hot pipes or vents), if you have planted only a small pot. If you start with a large propagating box, you can purchase a heating coil to spread on a one-inch layer of shredded styrofoam in the bottom before putting in the vermiculite; it should maintain 75°. One warning: If you use a heat cable, keep the medium around it damp when it is working so it won't burn out; don't let the vermiculite dry.

About the potting material: Sand and peat moss have been standbys for years. But vermiculite (*not* perlite) has proven more effective; it is clean and free of the fungi spores found in other mediums. Damp-off, the dread threat to young seedlings, is avoided.

When the first green appears, bring the container closer to light. Transplant after the first two pseudo-leaves ("cotyledons") appear. Use sterile tweezers to lift; put into a tiny pot of soilless mix, cover with plastic or glass for the first 10 days.

30

SOIL HEATING CABLES SUPPLY SAFE GENTLE BOTTOM HEAT TO START SEEDS, CUTTINGS

EXOTIC SEEDS

Exotic seeds require special cultural techniques, and the supplier should furnish information on the best method to propagate. Rare seed specialist John Brudy has a mixture that has worked well for me and I can recommend it. In his catalog, he offers seven different methods of propagation, depending on the seeds, which have proved most effective. He also suggests daily inspection of seed beds and seedlings. Some plants take six months or more to show signs of life, others will appear in one to three weeks. A time schedule is furnished for each seed so you'll know whether you can wait around long enough for it to graduate from college!

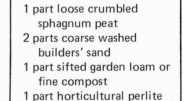

1 part loose crumbled
   sphagnum peat
2 parts coarse washed
   builders' sand
1 part sifted garden loam or
   fine compost
1 part horticultural perlite

31

**ADD A WINDOW
GREENHOUSE OUTSIDE
(COMMERCIAL UNITS
AVAILABLE)**

CARE AND FEEDING: PROPAGATION

SEED GROWING

Q *I seem to have a purple thumb when I try to get seeds to grow. Do you have any suggestions?*

A The planting medium may have been too heavy, or too wet. The propagating container needs bottom warmth to encourage the action; your pot may have taken cold. Also, seeds lose their urge to grow as they get older; look for a date on a package to be sure the seeds are this year's crop. If you salvaged the seeds from your own plants, don't make them wait.

Q *If I cover a seed bed with clear plastic should it be completely airtight?*

A No, a small amount of air circulation is essential; being able to lift the covering is necessary to check seeds, moisture. I would place the cover on loosely, or make a couple of small holes in the material if the cover is tight-fitting.

STERILIZING

Q *What can I use to sterilize small tools quickly?*

A Have a small jar of vinegar handy. Dip the knife or tweezers and shake off the excess.

TANGLED ROOTS

Q *Why do the roots of my seedlings get tangled? They're always hard to separate.*

A You've left them too long in the propagating box.

SOURCES OF SEEDS AND PLANTS

John Brudy's Rare Plant House, Box 1348, Cocoa Beach, FL 32931; catalog, $1; seeds, rare and tropical

Kartuz Greenhouses, Wilmington, MA 01887; catalog, 50 cents; gesneriads, begonias, etc.

Rod McLellan Orchids, 1450 El Camino Real, So. San Francisco, CA 94080

Geo. W. Park Seed Co., Greenwood, SC 29647

Roehr's Exotic Nurseries, R.F.D. 2, Box 144, Farmingdale, NJ 07727

Wayside Gardens, Mentor, OH 44060; catalog, $2; wide selection of seeds

White Flower Farm, Litchfield, CT 06759; catalog, $3; excellent growing information; seeds, plants

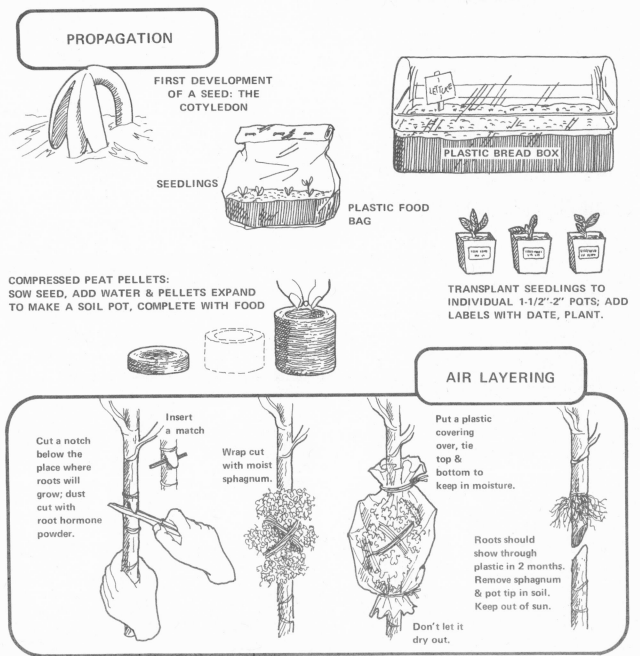

PROPAGATION

FIRST DEVELOPMENT OF A SEED: THE COTYLEDON

SEEDLINGS

PLASTIC FOOD BAG

PLASTIC BREAD BOX

LETTUCE

COMPRESSED PEAT PELLETS: SOW SEED, ADD WATER & PELLETS EXPAND TO MAKE A SOIL POT, COMPLETE WITH FOOD

TRANSPLANT SEEDLINGS TO INDIVIDUAL 1-1/2"-2" POTS; ADD LABELS WITH DATE, PLANT.

33

AIR LAYERING

Cut a notch below the place where roots will grow; dust cut with root hormone powder.

Insert a match

Wrap cut with moist sphagnum.

Put a plastic covering over, tie top & bottom to keep in moisture.

Don't let it dry out.

Roots should show through plastic in 2 months. Remove sphagnum & pot tip in soil. Keep out of sun.

CARE AND FEEDING: PROPAGATION

STOLONS

Creeping little-leaf greens send out runners, or stolons, which usually have a cluster of leaves out at the end. These are potential new plants, eventually developing independent root systems. They have no nodes, but are green (in the case of strawberries, red) extension cords.

STOLON

You can twist these stolons around the top of the pot's soil and pin down the plantlet with a hairpin or half a paper clip. *Episcia,* Spider plant and *Ficus repens* reproduce this way. Put a small pot filled with moistened packaged soil next to the parent pot; stretch the stolon so that the new plant is in the middle of the small pot and pin it down. It will root in 10 days and you can cut the connection. It is also possible to sever the stolon from the big plant, leaving about half an inch of the stolon, and to propagate it like a cutting.

LAYERING

This is the accredited way of making new plants from single-stem big ones. *Dieffenbachia,* self-heading *Philodendron, Dracaena,* croton and the *Ficus* family all lend themselves to this method rather than by means of stem cuttings. The main reason for tackling air layering is to solve the retirement age of tired big plants which no longer have any lower leaves. There are few sights sadder than a doddering *Dieffenbachia* with two droopy leaves at the top of a mangy stem.

Air layering is a means of making roots grow on stems close to the existing leaves, so that you can cut off the top of the plant and start another from the foreshortened tip. What's left can be tossed out; or, in the case of the Ti plant and *Dieffenbachia,* the lower portion of the stem can be cut in six- to twelve-inch lengths which in turn propagate new plants when started in moist sand or vermiculite both in a plastic-bag-covered pot. Keep the old stub out of sight, water it, and new leaves may start along the side in the form of offsets.

OFFSETS

Some plants like the succulents and bromeliads develop offsets, or suckers, at the base. These are miniature copies of the parent plant. *Agave, Aloe,* banana, begonias do it, as well as others. The offset can be cut off from the parent plant once it has developed serious roots; with a clean sharp knife cut as close to the main stem as possible and you can gently pull to get any roots. Pot up the offset in moistened sand and peat mixture, place inside a plastic bag to hold moisture, until it forms acceptable roots. The succulents should be allowed to callus, or harden the cut edges by being left out for a day or two before bagging.

RHIZOMES

Instead of the root systems most green things depend on, plants like *Achimenes* have a thickened underground stem that creeps along near the surface, and roots grow out of that. This rhizome can be long and slim, like the ones in lawn grasses, or fat and gnarled, as in some outdoor bulbs. *Achimenes* rhizomes develop scaly clusters. They respond to moisture, warmth and bright light. Once the flowering of the plant is through, the plant goes into decline, but that's just the beginning of yearly hibernation. Store rhizomes in plastic bags with a covering of peat and by late winter you can divide and increase the pot population for the following year.

TUBERS

Begonias, the most common tubers, are propagated generally by leaf cuttings, by rhizomes, and by tubers. This last group includes a Christmas begonia and a summer-blooming variety which do well under fluorescent light. The tubers can be bought, sometimes having little stem buds started. They should be planted, round end down, in peat kept moist but not soggy. Bottom heat will push them along, and once roots develop and stalks have leaves of uniform size, they can be lifted, being careful not to disturb the root ball, and placed in a pot of

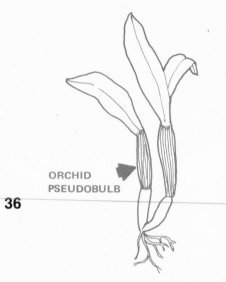

ORCHID
PSEUDOBULB

rich soil with the top of the tuber exposed. Continue to give them mild light, and a light fish-emulsion feeding; too much causes leaves to curl. Tubers are susceptible to mildew when too wet; they also want ventilation but shun drafts. Tuberous begonia growers are a special breed; they love the challenge of a difficult plant, yet will tell you raising begonias is *so* easy! So get interested at your own risk.

BULBS

Whole books are written on the care and propagation of the lily family. Suffice it to say that when you buy, look for the biggest and fattest of each variety. Pre-cooled bulbs, which have been specially chilled for a specified time, are intended for early indoor bloom. Because they are forced, count on only one year's show of bloom. Bulbs which can be grown above water on stones, like *Narcissus* and *Crocus* should be bought only after you select the ones with smooth onion-skin look and healthy bottom, or plate.

There are some lavish indoor bulbs worth investigating: *Veltheimia* is a winter bloomer with scores of one-inch flowers on stalks one to two feet tall. *Tulbaghia* blooms most of the year with fragrant pale lavender stars in clusters at the end of foot-long stalks. *Sprekelia,* Aztec lily, sends up a huge orchid-like red blossom in early spring. Nose around your favorite nursery and experiment with bulbs you've never seen. This can lead you into whole new sensations, and like the begoniaddicts, there are the bulb bewitched.

SPORES

Like growing plants from seeds, the propagation of ferns from spores, those little dots under the fern leaves in neat rows, takes infinite time and patience. You can get involved up to a year before you have a fern for potting. Before that time, they will need at least 20 hours daily of fluorescent light, temperature control of 70° and a daily misting of the surface. I personally enjoy the great beauty of the mature fern too much to wait for a spore to grow up. Spore growing is for specialists.

AIR LAYERING

Q *I have tried air layering my Dracaena because it was touching the ceiling. Two months have gone by and nothing has happened.*

A There could be several reasons; perhaps the cut wasn't deep enough, or the plastic was not tight enough and the sphagnum dried out. Check for moisture, and reset the plastic. Some plants are stubborn and take longer before deciding to root. However, a *Dracaena* should have made some roots in two months' period.

DIVIDING

Q *Can I divide an Aspidistra?*

A Yes. Plants with more than one stem usually can be separated. Water the *Aspidistra* the day before the "operation" with a vitamin B-1 solution to help it avoid transplant shock. Knock the plant out of the pot and with a sterile knife cut the plant in two or more sections.

OFFSETS

Q *When should I pot up an offset of my bromeliad?*

A If you don't mind the unattractive older plant which has had its blossoming and fulfilled its mission in life, it is a good idea to wait until the little plantlet has developed a good vase shape. Bromeliads like tight conditions, so start it in a four-inch clay pot.

RHIZOMES

Q *Do ferns ever have rhizomes?*

A One family, called the *Davallia,* does have visibly growing rhizomes which are covered with a furry kind of growth. These spread over the edges of pots and are the reason for common names like Rabbit's Foot or Squirrel's Foot ferns.

TUBERS

Q *I have an Oxalis plant which a friend shared with me. It has big triangular leaves which fold at night. Can it be divided?*

A Sounds like you have *Oxalis regnelli.* This is a tuberous plant and new tubers reproduce rapidly. Remove the plant from its pot and shake off all loose soil; wash off the rest, then separate the tiny tubers. Put them in a container with an inch layer of moist vermiculite, spreading them around. Cover with another half inch of the moist vermiculite and set the box in a shaded spot without covering. New tubers will start sprouting and can be potted.

37

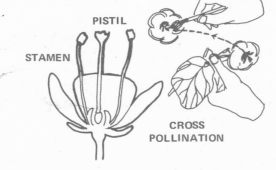

PISTIL

STAMEN

CROSS POLLINATION

WATER: THE WARM BOTTLE

There are people who water their ferns with beer and there are those who put leftover ice cubes on crotons. I have a feeling that those same people are the kind who insist on adding ginger ale to Scotch.

Water is nature's liquid. Warm it and you bring the living green as close to the condition of its place of origin as you can, taking into consideration the additives which flow out of faucets along with the water. Even rainwater is weighted with particles of pollutants, but plants show greater tolerances for rainwater than for municipal water. Maybe beer *does* give a tired Mother fern a lift, but to date I can't prove the theory. As for ice cubes: Drop one down the back of anyone who does that to a plant!

Verified tests prove that cold water slows growth, warm speeds it. Specifically, the Danbury School of Horticulture, Danbury, Connecticut, found that "warming the water to an optimum temperature of 90° speeded the cells' characteristics above normal growth until the soil's cooling effect slowed reaction to normal, or about five hours." Additional tests made at Michigan State University and by the States of Oregon and Washington underline the accuracy of this information. Horticulturists suggest, too, that warming water helps quicken rooting of transplants. In the individual case histories of house plants in this book the word "tepid" appears again and again to remind you: Never put a chill on your green friendship. One more suggestion about tepid water. Liquid plant foods diluted in it and administered are used more efficiently by the plant.

Our teeth may be more resistant to decay because of the addition of fluorine in water. But that same chemical seems to set teeth on edge for members of the *Agave, Maranta* and lily families. Tip browning and spots on leaves have been traced to this. Some cities use heavier amounts, causing even more concern in green circles. Rainwater is the safest, cheapest answer; bottled water is a second choice. Sphagnum peat and perlite contain minute amounts of fluorine; when starting cuttings or seeds, tepid rainwater is the safe way to grow.

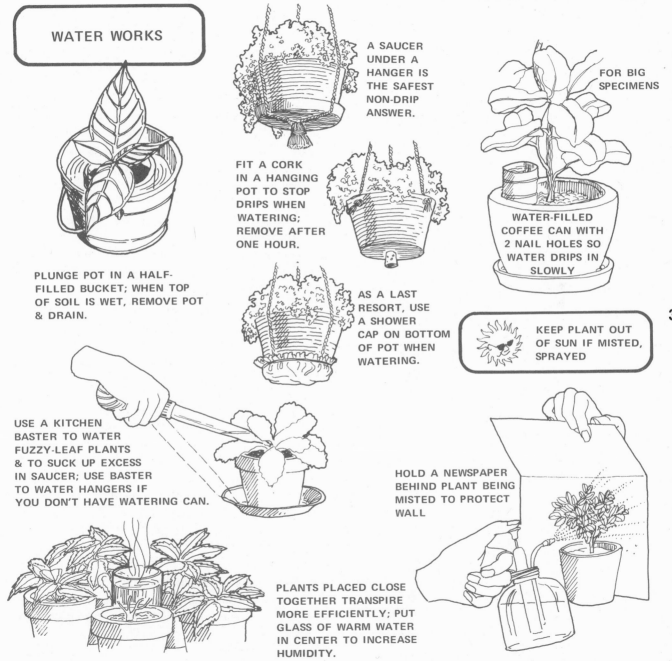

WATER WORKS

PLUNGE POT IN A HALF-FILLED BUCKET; WHEN TOP OF SOIL IS WET, REMOVE POT & DRAIN.

A SAUCER UNDER A HANGER IS THE SAFEST NON-DRIP ANSWER.

FIT A CORK IN A HANGING POT TO STOP DRIPS WHEN WATERING; REMOVE AFTER ONE HOUR.

AS A LAST RESORT, USE A SHOWER CAP ON BOTTOM OF POT WHEN WATERING.

FOR BIG SPECIMENS

WATER-FILLED COFFEE CAN WITH 2 NAIL HOLES SO WATER DRIPS IN SLOWLY

KEEP PLANT OUT OF SUN IF MISTED, SPRAYED

39

USE A KITCHEN BASTER TO WATER FUZZY-LEAF PLANTS & TO SUCK UP EXCESS IN SAUCER; USE BASTER TO WATER HANGERS IF YOU DON'T HAVE WATERING CAN.

HOLD A NEWSPAPER BEHIND PLANT BEING MISTED TO PROTECT WALL

PLANTS PLACED CLOSE TOGETHER TRANSPIRE MORE EFFICIENTLY; PUT GLASS OF WARM WATER IN CENTER TO INCREASE HUMIDITY.

CARE AND FEEDING: WATER

"TOO MUCH WATER? . . . NOT ENOUGH?"

The first question an inexperienced plant parent asks of the plant shop owner is: "How often do I water it?" Not even green thumbers can answer that. Conditions in a home can't be like those in the plant shop, or even the greenhouse where it first saw light. Watering is a learned art. Plants give signals, and you have to learn to recognize, "Daddy, I'm thirsty!"

It's dangerous to generalize but I would say that most house plants are comfortable with a thorough watering and are then allowed to become slightly moist before watering again. The roots work to reach the moisture as it recedes and the plant flourishes. If the soil is saturated without waiting for this drying-out period, and the roots can't get oxygen because water fills up all the spaces, the signal to watch for is leaves which start yellowing, and edges turning brown.

SLIGHTLY MOIST

That phrase is difficult to explain. If the soil mixture feels damp like a squeezed-out face cloth, that's "slightly moist." The soil will still be darker than when it is dry. And your finger poked down into the mixture is the final indication of whether it's time to water or not. Loose plant mixtures may be bone dry for a depth of one or two inches, but quite wet below; don't let the dry look tempt you to irrigate before you should.

Soft stem plants like Piggyback should never dry out entirely; forget to water and you might as well go out and buy a new one. Hydrangeas and *Impatiens* leaves droop straight down when they're signaling—and pop back when they have a drink.

For the first few days of being a foster plant parent it is good practice to touch the soil with your index finger once a day. Take note of the room temperature: Is it the same all the time? A cooler period and the plant uses less water; if it suddenly heats up, you may have to water twice as often.

LOOK FOR WATERING POT WITH LONG SLIM SPOUT

HOOD NECESSARY TO KEEP WATER FROM SPILLING

CURVE BAD: DRIPS OUT OF TOP

Contrary to popular notion, succulents and cacti need water; everything has to have moisture to exist. Desert types can go all winter without a drink. The Pencil cactus takes more water than you'd expect in spring and summer.

"How much water?" "When do I water?" It depends on the plant and its personal needs, where the plant rooms, what kind of a pot it sits in, what the hot/cold conditions are, how much light it gets. Remember, when you're not sure, experts make bad guesses too.

HUMID ERROR

In all probability, your adopted young green was born in a greenhouse where temperature and humidity were nursery controlled. You brought it home and the thermometer shows a comfort range of 68° to 72°, for both of you. But, the humidity—that's the sticky bit. Living for you can be unpleasant when moisture content of the air is high enough to please the "baby."

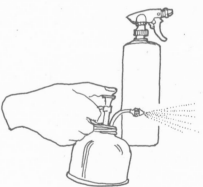

So you compromise. You mist or you spray. Misting is a fine burst of water from a mister or fogger which splits drops into hundreds of almost invisible droplets. A spray is the steady flow of streams of water from a shower head, a kitchen dish spray or a yard hose. Some plants like orchids tolerate misting but shun heavy water on the leaves. Misting ups humidity, spraying is closer to taking a shower.

Perhaps the simplest "upper" for humidity is the shallow tray filled with pebbles and set under a pot; the pebbles are moistened, but not to the top of the layer because no pot should sit in water—unless it is a true water-baby. "Pebbles" can be any number of materials: river-washed stones, granite or marble chips, polished beach stones, Japanese fish-tank pebbles. The water furnishes the humidity as it evaporates. There is a waffle-crating of plastic available in larger sheets which can be cut to fit the tray: it's easy to clean and holds the pot above the water.

Grouping plants together develops a nice community empathy. They help one another by transpiring more efficiently. Add a glass of warm water in the middle of the group to push humidity even higher.

CARE AND FEEDING: WATER

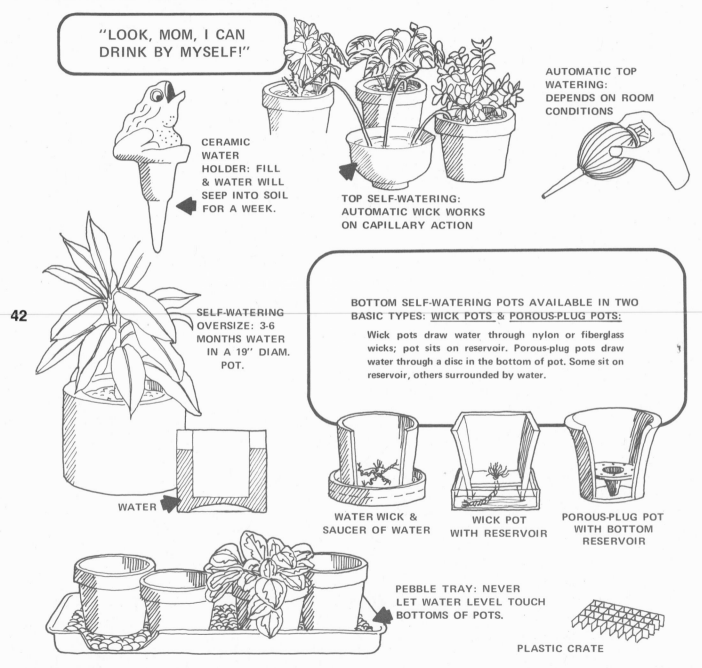

"LOOK, MOM, I CAN DRINK BY MYSELF!"

CERAMIC WATER HOLDER: FILL & WATER WILL SEEP INTO SOIL FOR A WEEK.

TOP SELF-WATERING: AUTOMATIC WICK WORKS ON CAPILLARY ACTION

AUTOMATIC TOP WATERING: DEPENDS ON ROOM CONDITIONS

SELF-WATERING OVERSIZE: 3-6 MONTHS WATER IN A 19" DIAM. POT.

BOTTOM SELF-WATERING POTS AVAILABLE IN TWO BASIC TYPES: WICK POTS & POROUS-PLUG POTS:

Wick pots draw water through nylon or fiberglass wicks; pot sits on reservoir. Porous-plug pots draw water through a disc in the bottom of pot. Some sit on reservoir, others surrounded by water.

WATER

WATER WICK & SAUCER OF WATER

WICK POT WITH RESERVOIR

POROUS-PLUG POT WITH BOTTOM RESERVOIR

PEBBLE TRAY: NEVER LET WATER LEVEL TOUCH BOTTOMS OF POTS.

PLASTIC CRATE

DRAINAGE

Because drainage is so critical, it is worth repeating the need for efficient removal of moisture. Uncrocked pots get clogged, so promise you'll crock every time you repot. And if you double-pot, a smaller pot inside a larger one, don't forget to lift up the planted pot to be sure water isn't collecting in the lower one. A friend's palm looked like the ugly stepsister until we discovered the lower jar held two inches of smelly water which had accumulated.

SELF-WATERING SCHEMES

Many nurserymen depend on a water wick, inserted in the drainage hole in the bottom, to water flowering plants like African violets. You can buy this wicking at a nursery, cut it to the length you want and let capillary action solve some of your plant's time-taking demands. Also, there are several commercial self waterers available now which will water plants from the top by means of a ceramic gadget connected by tube to a container of water. The gadget waters the plant when it gets a message: I'm dry. You can water plants for a couple of weeks this way.

FLORA-GROW AUTOMATIC DRAINAGE FOR POTS WITHOUT DRAIN HOLES; CAPILLARY ACTION MOVES WATER UP & OUT

43

BATTERY-OPERATED GREEN THUMB PLANT COMMUNICATOR: TELLS YOU WHEN WATERING IS NEEDED

SAV-A-PLANT GIVES READINGS OF MOISTURE AT VARIOUS LEVELS; 9" PROBE EXCELLENT FOR BIG CONTAINERS

CARE AND FEEDING: WATER

BUCKET WATERING

Q *I have a plant which was potted with the soil right up to the top and it's hard to water.*

A If you can't scrape away any of the soil, fill a bucket halfway with tepid water and set the pot in it to seep through the bottom. Once bubbles come through the top, you know you've watered thoroughly. Some day, when you have time, repot the plant.

EGG WATER

Q *Is it true the water I use to boil eggs will benefit some of my plants?*

A Yes, cooled water contains lime, and anti-acid plants will be pleased to accept. Room temperature tea will furnish a treat to acid-loving greens.

CHLORINE

Q *Our city water is heavily chlorinated. Have you any suggestions other than rainwater or bottled water for my plants?*

A If it is difficult to collect rainwater, draw a container from your faucet and let it stand overnight before using. Softened water is bad for plants, too, because sodium used to soften is injurious; don't use.

WINTER WATERING

Q *Why do my plants need less water in winter? They're still growing, aren't they?*

A Nature slows down indoors just like it does outdoors. Almost all plants go through this cycle; their growth slows to a snail's pace, and they need less food and water until the sap starts running in spring.

HANGER WATERING

Q *Why do my hanging ferns seem to need more water than the one on my bathroom counter?*

A Any heat in a room rises, so the hanging plants are in a warmer, dryer condition than the one in the bath. Also, air is circulating all around the hangers and drying-out action is faster.

FUZZY-LEAF WATERING

Q *Is there any way to water fuzzy-leaf plants besides submerging the bottom of the pot?*

A A kitchen baster with its tiny point sneaked between the leaves will let you water the top. The whole point is to keep water from brown-spotting the velvety leaves.

TERRARIUMS

Q *If a terrarium keeps moist plants growing, I don't see any reason for water gardens.*

A Terrariums are really enclosed soil and sand gardens, home base for limited-size plants. The water garden grows in non-soil conditions, gets all its nourishment from fertilized water. It is an open container which allows the plant to grow to any size it chooses. Also, it is much easier to complete than complicated bottle terrariums with tight necks.

VACATIONS

Q *If I'm gone for a week, how will I keep the water level up on my water gardens?*

A Similarly to proven vacation treatment: Enclose the container and plant in a plastic bag; if the leaves are tall, use a cleaner's clothing bag cover. Set the container out of sunlight.

METAL CONTAINERS

Q *Can I make a water garden out of an old copper tea kettle?*

A Copper, brass or any container with lead lining should not be used because chemicals in the fertilizer react negatively.

GRASSES

Q *Are there some small grasses I could try in water?*

A Mondo grass, *Ophiopogon japonicus* and *Liriope* will form handsome clumps of dark-green strap leaves. If they get some sun, you may get masses of pretty blue flowers.

DRAINING EXCESS WATER

Q *Why can't I fill the water level to the top of the dish if it's a water plant?*

A Because the roots need some oxygen and this is the only way they can get it. If the plant looks unhappy two weeks after planting, remove some of the fertilized water—it may be shutting off oxygen. Big containers are hard to empty: Try a flexible plastic tube and syphon off the water. Fill the tube from the faucet; cover ends with thumbs so no air escapes. Lower one end into the planter, keeping thumb tightly on the other end until you have it right into the sink drain. Drain end has to be lower than planter end.

45

PLANTED LARGE
FISH BOWL; PLACE A TALL
CLEAR VASE INSIDE &
WATER-PLANT LIRIOPE.

WEANING: FEEDING

More house plants have expired because their foster parents tried to stuff them with food. I have watched people measure out a teaspoon of fish emulsion, and then toss in an extra spoonful "for good measure." If only there were a Dr. Spock for green babies to say *"Don't overfeed!"*

Plants just home from the nursery have been force-fed to look their best so you couldn't resist their cute style. For that reason, wait four to six months before you start spoon-feeding. When a plant grows in semi-shade or modest light too much food may also produce heartburn at the roots, and there's no Digel which can help that. Plants which naturally grow slowly should not be forced to keep up with others.

There is no substitute for proper moisture, good light and temperature; feeding a pot which isn't feeling up to it will *not* correct other weaknesses, and only makes it sicker. Also, an overfed plant doesn't have time to build its natural strengths; stems are too thin for the bigger leaves, branches produce more leaves than the roots can handle.

There are dozens of good house-plant foods available. Fish emulsion, the liquid form, is dependable, no matter how long it has been opened. The pellet forms, the powders, the tablets are all efficient. Most important, rather than the physical shape, is the formula: Look for those three numbers so you know what you're getting. The label 10-20-10 is a balanced diet for most plants; as long as the middle number is twice the other two, it will give the plant adequate *phosphorus*, or *phosphates*, which build up the sturdy cell growth and are boosts to blooms. The first 10 stands for *nitrogen* which makes things green, like grass. The last 10 is for *potassium* which balances the nitrogen and stiffens the stems as well as discouraging bugs.

Just remember, half the amount of food recommended by the manufacturer is the safest way to wean your green. And always give it a drink *before* feeding.

ACID PLANTS

Q *Do acid-loving plants take any special additives?*

A They do best with about equal amounts of nitrogen and phosphorus, but want a higher dose of potassium, and iron chelate.

BONEMEAL

Q *I use bonemeal in my garden. Can I use it on indoor plants?*

A *On* house plants? No. But *yes,* mixed into the soil in small quantities, organic feedings of about a tablespoon to a gallon pail of soil will give a big phosphorus lift, but no nitrogen and only a trace of potassium. (Fish emulsion is heavy in nitrogen, that's why it's good for big greenies.)

LIGHT FEEDING

Q *Do plants grown indoors under lights take more feeding than those grown in daylight?*

A The accelerated growth under lights puts more demands on photosynthesis (that's a combination of all the plant's forces to produce singular results by means of sunlight or artificial light). They will take more moisture, and adding a dilute amount of food each time you water will give the young things a shot in the stomata.

NAP TIME

Q *I was told not to feed house plants during their rest period. When does that time start?*

A When the plant stops growing, usually in November, depending on the climate where you live. In warm areas like the south, a very light feeding all year round won't harm because tropical conditions foster continual growth.

ORGANIC VS CHEMICAL FOODS

Q *I'm just a beginner, but I refuse to use chemicals on plants. Is there organic plant food?*

Fish emulsion and bonemeal are naturals for you. They add trace elements needed plus goodies your plants love. But as long as these plants aren't food greens, don't write off the chemicals: Formulas specially made for certain plants like orchids and violets can't be matched by organics.

SICK PLANTS

Q *Why can't I feed a plant which has mealy bug?*

A That's a real Plant Mother question: Don't do it because I say don't do it! (All plant experts say it too, so it must be a valid answer.) When a plant is sick or diseased, hold off on its feed. The plant is busy fighting for its life and the roots can't assimilate any overload at this time.

SPRAY FEEDING

Q *I have friends who spray fertilizer on the leaves of their plants. Is this something I should try?*

A I prefer direct root feeding for the plants I've adopted with the exception of two families: orchids and bromeliads. These were epiphitic, or tree-growing plants in their native state, and they absorbed food through aerial roots and leaves because they weren't in touch with the ground. A mild feeding, perhaps one-fourth normal amount of fertilizer to water, can be sprayed to advantage in addition to regular watering. Bromeliads want their distinctive "vase" to be filled, as well as leaves sprayed. One additional exception to spraying food on leaves: If an acid-loving plant, like the lemon, has a jaundiced look, and chelated iron is fed into the roots, spraying some of the solution on the leaves increases action.

CARE AND FEEDING: FEEDING

TABLET FOOD

Q *You mention liquid plant food often, like fish emulsion. Is it better than the tablet form?*

A No. Each food has its own components, and I have depended on the liquid for many years because it was handy, and it worked. However, in the past two years marvelous developments have been made in this field. Timed-release tablets which will give a plant its whole year supply at one time has changed the entire food picture. There are so many on the market, I suggest you shop like a consumer advocate and decide for yourself. Your green friends may end up looking better than mine!

VITAMINS

Q *I hear that I should be giving my plants vitamins. Do I share mine?*

A Don't try your vitamins on the green scene: Roots have different digestive tracts than yours. Likewise, don't reverse the intake: Plant vitamin B-1 is loaded with additives which are harmful to your innards. The efficiency of this compound is debatable but I use it when I transplant, when I start cuttings, and the results make it worth suggesting. During the transplant operation, particularly of larger ones like citrus, tree forms and ornamentals (azaleas, camellias, gardenias, etc.), B-1 alleviates shock. Put two tablespoons of liquid B-1 which also contains iron, zinc, maganese and chelating agents, into one gallon of water and saturate the soil immediately after planting. Soaking cuttings in a one-tablespoon-to-a-quart-of-water solution, 30 minutes before planting, gives a boost.

WATER GARDEN FEEDING

Q *Is there any special fertilizer needed for feeding my water garden?*

A It should be a complete food, containing the Big Three (nitrogen, phosphorus and potassium) and additional iron, manganese and zinc. Check labels to be sure of serving full six-course meals.

HOT AIR: TEMPERATURE AND AIR CIRCULATION

Today, do something nice for your foster *Ficus.* Turn down the heat. Much is written about the importance of not over- or underwatering while the critical factor of heat has been minimized. It's really the first thing to solve after you sign the adoption papers. Of course, the amount and kind of light have to be considered eventually, but a new plant in the house will react faster to too much heat than to light or water. Purchasers of large house plants need to be reminded: Big leaves show agitation quickly, so keep a daily watch. Young small-leaf plants take longer to complain.

There are succulents and cacti and tropicals who relish warmth. But the majority of the green children would like a comfort zone somewhat cooler than your personal thermostat may acknowledge. Finding a temperature in which you can both operate is a right-now decision. Finding a nice balance which won't fluctuate during the day due to a miserly landlord or a prolonged energy crisis is like turning over a new leaf and finding green gold. Most plants prefer a steady-as-you-go 65° to 70° warmth, nighttime temperatures of 10 degrees less, and moving air. They get uneasy when one hour is warm, the next cool.

Most indoor plants can stand cool rooms, even in daytime, without serious damage. It is the heavy non-moving air in an overheated room that does them in. The advent of the air conditioner has saved many green lives. Unfortunately nothing is perfect, and some of these gadgets give out a deadly cold blast instead of moderated air; check yours so it won't send a friend into obit.

Moving air, gentle movement, is a great boon. Cross drafts from open doors and windows are *not* acceptable and can permanently retard a plant. Greenhouses have fans to keep the circulation active; this movement is a deterrent to the bug population, too. Natural summer heat can be countered with additional moisture and humidity. See the section on watering for suggestions.

INEXPENSIVE THERMOMETER
TO CHECK ROOM TEMPERATURE

ELECTRIC RESULTS: ARTIFICIAL LIGHTS

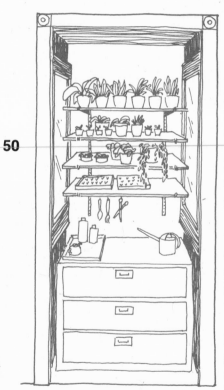

CLOSET PLANTER:
Build vertical frames
to hold 48″ fluores-
cent tubes; add a sheet
of translucent glass or
plastic in front of tubes
to cut glare.

Bringing up one house plant is a cinch: It gets the best window seat in the house, with no competition. But no family raises only one these days—20 or a hundred is more like it! The green scene has changed our life styles, our thinking about sharing space, because it gets first dibs on *light*. Our houses and apartments have limited light sources, windows. Often they're north when plants want the sun, or south when we collect shade-lovers. Houses with skylights, modern structures with glass walls or old houses with windows in all four sides get better breaks.

Fortunately there are things happening which will make even dark corners light up a plant's photosynthesis. Fluorescent artificial light for plant-growing has been around for at least 40 years. But only in the past year has a unit appeared which looks like the answer to a mainten-ance prayer: *Verilux Tru-Bloom,* manufactured by Verilux, Inc., Green-wich, Connecticut. Until this one came on the scene, fluorescent lights have been efficient, particularly after the combination of cool-white and warm-white proved successful over older combinations. But they added glare and distortion; even with baffles, the eye was caught.

In order to produce lights which would sell fast and in big quanti-ties to growers, manufacturers sacrificed naturalness for quick growth and bloom. Basically, those fluorescents were designed for agricultural growers, and house-plant use was a by-product. Unless the grower was knowledgeable, an African violet could get out of hand and become a tall skinny instead of blooming in a classic flat rosette.

What Tru-Bloom does for plant parents is bring natural light to the home environment at last. It gives out barely noticeable light, and the glare is not offensive. The colors of leaves and flowers are not distorted as with ordinary fluorescents. You can almost believe that it is *natural* light. With this low-visibility intensity, greens do not reach for the light, they sit and enjoy. Even plants which have been grown under cool fluorescent lights seem to respond with new pleasure—almost as if they have been given the choice window seat.

The catch? It is still not easy to locate this lamp, and then only in case lots from the manufacturer, Verilux, Inc. (round up light-growing

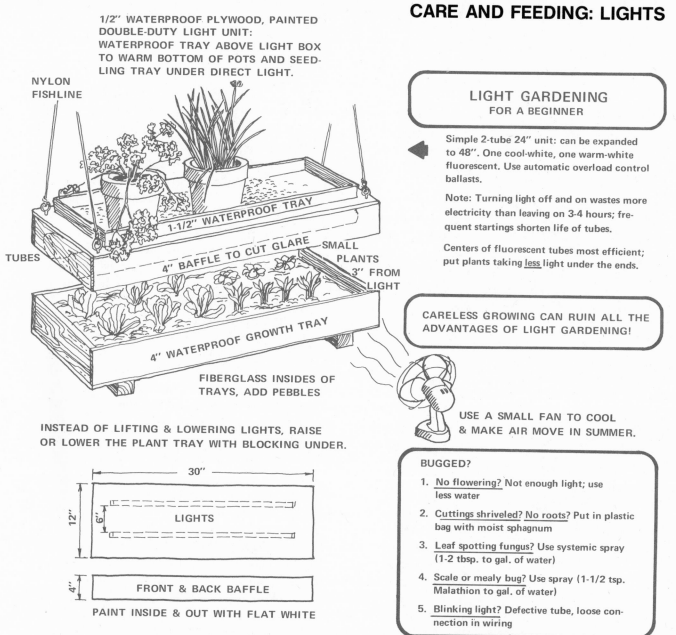

1/2" WATERPROOF PLYWOOD, PAINTED DOUBLE-DUTY LIGHT UNIT: WATERPROOF TRAY ABOVE LIGHT BOX TO WARM BOTTOM OF POTS AND SEEDLING TRAY UNDER DIRECT LIGHT.

NYLON FISHLINE

TUBES

1-1/2" WATERPROOF TRAY

4" BAFFLE TO CUT GLARE

SMALL PLANTS 3" FROM LIGHT

4" WATERPROOF GROWTH TRAY

FIBERGLASS INSIDES OF TRAYS, ADD PEBBLES

INSTEAD OF LIFTING & LOWERING LIGHTS, RAISE OR LOWER THE PLANT TRAY WITH BLOCKING UNDER.

30"

12"

6"

LIGHTS

4"

FRONT & BACK BAFFLE

PAINT INSIDE & OUT WITH FLAT WHITE

LIGHT GARDENING
FOR A BEGINNER

Simple 2-tube 24" unit: can be expanded to 48". One cool-white, one warm-white fluorescent. Use automatic overload control ballasts.

Note: Turning light off and on wastes more electricity than leaving on 3-4 hours; frequent startings shorten life of tubes.

Centers of fluorescent tubes most efficient; put plants taking less light under the ends.

CARELESS GROWING CAN RUIN ALL THE ADVANTAGES OF LIGHT GARDENING!

51

USE A SMALL FAN TO COOL & MAKE AIR MOVE IN SUMMER.

BUGGED?

1. No flowering? Not enough light; use less water

2. Cuttings shriveled? No roots? Put in plastic bag with moist sphagnum

3. Leaf spotting fungus? Use systemic spray (1-2 tbsp. to gal. of water)

4. Scale or mealy bug? Use spray (1-1/2 tsp. Malathion to gal. of water)

5. Blinking light? Defective tube, loose connection in wiring

RULE: When light level is low, keep soil on dry side, keep room cool, keep food to minimum. With more light, higher levels of these three will be acceptable to house plants.

CARE AND FEEDING: LIGHTS

RECYCLE THE
CABINET OF AN
EARLY TV WITH
LIGHTS & FERNS.

52

CLEAN OUT AN
UNUSED
FIREPLACE;
ADD A LIGHT BOX.

enthusiasts and pool your needs). The sizes are standard and typical; the lights are also somewhat more expensive. But they will last up to two years, cutting down normal replacement, and they deliver plant growth efficiency of 80 percent without loss of color-rendering ability. The source of this information is George Elbert, leader in the field of indoor light gardening, from an article in that outstanding house plant magazine, *Plants Alive.*

Until Tru-Bloom and other new light developments are readily available, cool-white and warm-white fluorescents in tandem will still be good friends to your young green family. Fluorescents give a total environmental control; there is no fluctuating of light like the now-you-see-it-now-you-don't sun. You can put plants where you want them for as long as you want. Seedlings, cuttings and vegetable starts respond 10 to 50 times better than those depending on an erratic-weather spring. Seeds of annuals and perennials can be started later, are ready earlier, for repotting or planting outdoors.

If the source of fluorescence is in a ceiling and a distance from plants, additional lighting time will compensate for the lessened intensity. When growing directly under lights, you can use a rule of green thumb, unofficial but workable, to decide how much light you need: 20 watts for each square foot of growing area for green-leaf things, 40 watts per square foot for flowering plants. Raising lights away from plants cuts down efficiency, lowering gives more. Sheets of open-waffled plastic baffles are available to install below the bulbs for balance and glare control.

There are cool floodlights, Cool Lux and Cool Beam, which can be used for the single large plant. Experts do not agree on their efficiency, but one spotlight, well-placed, can give encouragement and importance to an unlighted specimen. These lights *must* be used with ceramic sockets, not in ordinary lamp outlets because they can be fire hazards—the heat of the lamp is reflected back toward the socket. GE and Sylvania make these two lamps.

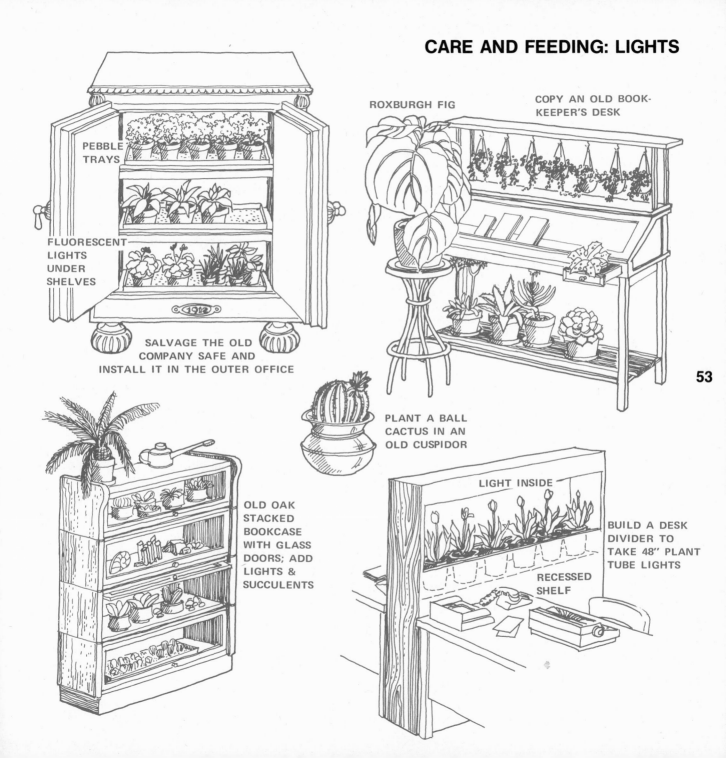

PEBBLE TRAYS

FLUORESCENT LIGHTS UNDER SHELVES

SALVAGE THE OLD COMPANY SAFE AND INSTALL IT IN THE OUTER OFFICE

ROXBURGH FIG

COPY AN OLD BOOK-KEEPER'S DESK

PLANT A BALL CACTUS IN AN OLD CUSPIDOR

OLD OAK STACKED BOOKCASE WITH GLASS DOORS; ADD LIGHTS & SUCCULENTS

LIGHT INSIDE

BUILD A DESK DIVIDER TO TAKE 48" PLANT TUBE LIGHTS

RECESSED SHELF

If you have one of those high-intensity desk lamps, the Tensor-type, you might try it on some of your cacti. Growth of a small *Echeveria* has been upped 25 percent on a 12-hour-per-day schedule. The light's heat is double that of incandescents, so don't put the cacti too close.

One artificial light problem to be dealt with: the "pollution" in cities from sodium vapor street lights. The red rays disturb trees which, having been encouraged by the rays to keep their leaves on, shun dormancy in fall, and then suffer when the first cold spell hits. House plants in windows facing these lights react abnormally in the winter resting period so pull your curtains at night if you haven't before.

CHILDREN OF NATURAL LIGHT

Something to think about if your plants are growing in nature's light: Dirty windows can cut light as much as a third, and adopting more plants should give you incentive you need to do that put-off job! The flat faces of leaves turn toward bright light; for this reason plants in or near a window must be rotated so each leaf gets a fair chance. A professor in New Zealand found that rotating his plants counter-clockwise made them happy, while doing it clockwise confused them. I turn mine at least every two weeks, but have had no complaints when I forget and turn *with* the clock.

Winter sun is cool; no-sun-in-summer greens will be pepped up by full sun in winter time. Summer light is bright and hot. Plan to move your family of plants around—out of the sun if they prefer filtered light, into the sun if they like a warm summer. This moving also gives you new arrangements—and a chance to look over each plant carefully to see if it has a dirty neck and needs a bath, or is bugged.

ENERGY CRISIS

Q *During the energy crisis last year, I turned off all my plant lights, and of course I lost most of the plants. I wonder how much electricity was saved.*

A Fluorescents use much less energy than incandescent lights. And if you had cut back on things like three-way lamps, TV, toasters, dishwashers, you could have saved your plants; these appliances are all high wattage pieces of equipment.

INCANDESCENT LIGHTS

Q *I leave a light on in my hall all day because it is too dark. Will that light be enough to keep a Kangaroo Treebine alive?*

A Much depends on the wattage of the light, but if it is a 75-watt lamp and the plant is within three feet, say as a hanging basket, it will live. The vine won't grow appreciably; however, you probably have to leave it on all through the evening, so the additional time will help it survive.

LEAVES CURL

Q *I've just started an indoor light garden, but I'm worried because some of the leaves are curling under.*

A That happens when the plant is too close to the light or is getting too much brightness.

LANKY VINES

Q *I have some vines on a north enclosed porch. They all seem leggy with the leaves far apart, and they are discouraging to look at. What is wrong?*

A Sorry, not enough light. Why don't you take cuttings from the ones which still look like they have life, and then revise the porch by adding two 48-inch fluorescent lights. When you pot the cuttings, they should begin to grow naturally in the added brightness. Plants inherit certain family patterns and even though we change some of them by neglect, they revert back to their inherited rhythm when the conditions are favorable.

REFLECTED LIGHT

Q *If I paint the wall behind my plants with glossy white will that reflected light help?*

A White is excellent, but stay with a flat white paint. The reflection from hot sun on high gloss can be too much for the plants.

SUNNY WINDOW BLOOMERS

Q *I am retired and I have a sunny window I enjoy. Is there any plant which can stand sun, and keep blooming all year around?*

A One of the *Euphorbia*, Crown of Thorns, is a year-round bloomer, but it is poisonous, and I can't recommend it. Why don't you consider several plants, rotating as they come into bloom? The Firecracker vine, lantana, marguerites, poinsettia, bromeliads are easy to keep during the non-bloom period in a holding pattern while the bloomer lands in the window. If you can find an electrician, supplemental light could be added to the window to take care of rainy and wintery days. A two-tube fluorescent unit with a reflector will lengthen short daylight. Use one cool-white and one warm-white tube; for encouraging bloom, consider the Gro-Lux Wide Spectrum. The fixture should not be more than 18 inches above.

WATER SPOTS ON LEAVES

Q *If I spill water on the leaves of plants under lights, will that damage the leaves like sunlight does?*

A Artificial light doesn't cause water-mark leaves.

PICKING UP AFTER THE KIDS: PLANTKEEPING

GENTLY WASH AN
OLD MAN CACTUS
IN SOAPY WATER,
RINSE & BLOW DRY.

TOP-DRESSING

CAREFULLY REMOVE A LAYER
OF SOIL FROM TOP OF POT
AND REPLACE WITH FRESH
SOIL TO ORIGINAL DEPTH

Plantkeeping is a good word for the small chores of a plant parent. Dead blossoms need to be removed; the soil should be pushed in place from the top inside of the pot where heavy watering pushed it. The outside of a clay pot can stand a wire brushing about every six months to bring back its newness.

Like the first haircut, a branch trim may upset you more than the child (plants are not supposed to mind it, I'm told). You'll be doing the spindly long branches a favor, encouraging them to grow stronger, thicker. Even a pinching of the tips to take out a few leaves is like a little love pat that will animate positive growth.

Plantkeeping takes in things like adding stakes or supports if your green leans toward you. It includes the all-important cleanliness, like washing a fern under the shower, or gently sponging the dust off each leaf of the Fiddle Leaf fig, or removing dried leaf sheaths of a palm.

If the bare soil under a large plant annoys you, add a mulch of white quartz chips or a layer of beach pebbles (thoroughly washed to remove any salt); these will also add light reflection for the undersides of leaves above. Or try a planting of ground cover like Creeping fig to soften the edge of the container. If it's an old plant which has been in its pot for a long time, a top-dressing will do something nice for tired topsoil. Take an old spoon and scrape away the upper one to two inches of soil, working around roots carefully; replace the discarded with soil as nearly like it as possible. Add half a teaspoon of bonemeal and some peat moss for stimulant and give a thorough watering; see what a good parent you are!

Plantkeeping is also the constant watchfulness of a parent checking for symptoms of childhood diseases—before they get serious. A moment to look under leaves, to check for yellowing, to note any undue stickiness from predators will save plantaches later.

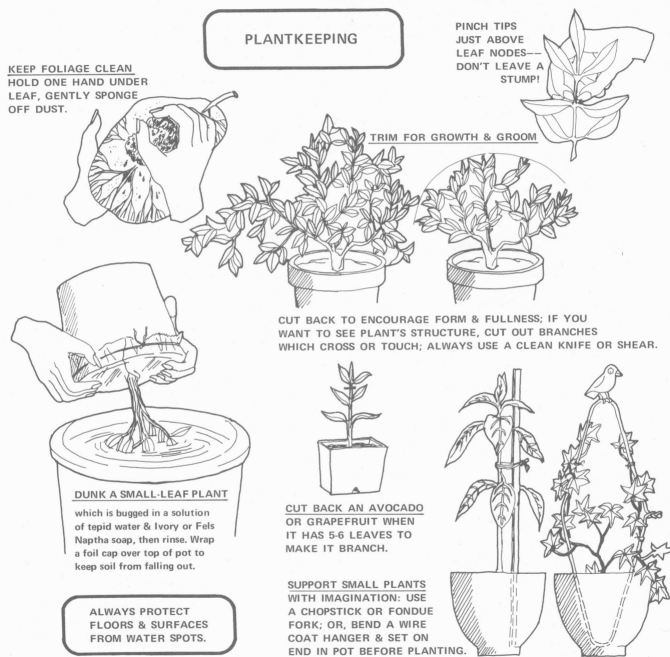

PLANTKEEPING

PINCH TIPS JUST ABOVE LEAF NODES—DON'T LEAVE A STUMP!

KEEP FOLIAGE CLEAN
HOLD ONE HAND UNDER LEAF, GENTLY SPONGE OFF DUST.

TRIM FOR GROWTH & GROOM

CUT BACK TO ENCOURAGE FORM & FULLNESS; IF YOU WANT TO SEE PLANT'S STRUCTURE, CUT OUT BRANCHES WHICH CROSS OR TOUCH; ALWAYS USE A CLEAN KNIFE OR SHEAR.

DUNK A SMALL-LEAF PLANT
which is bugged in a solution of tepid water & Ivory or Fels Naptha soap, then rinse. Wrap a foil cap over top of pot to keep soil from falling out.

CUT BACK AN AVOCADO OR GRAPEFRUIT WHEN IT HAS 5-6 LEAVES TO MAKE IT BRANCH.

SUPPORT SMALL PLANTS
WITH IMAGINATION: USE A CHOPSTICK OR FONDUE FORK; OR, BEND A WIRE COAT HANGER & SET ON END IN POT BEFORE PLANTING.

ALWAYS PROTECT FLOORS & SURFACES FROM WATER SPOTS.

ANYONE-CAN-GROW-THEM PLANTS

CHINESE EVERGREEN

SWEDISH IVY

PINK POLKADOT

AGAVE

OLD MILK CAN LACQUERED; ADD DECAL

Plant collectors, if you'll excuse the all-inclusive phrase, are snobs like book people and bird people: When a thing is common or easy to find, it's a bore. They wouldn't be caught green-handed coming out of a planterie with a Piggyback. That doesn't mean purchasing a Piggyback is a social blunder. In fact, there are probably more P-b's in circulation today than there are plant collectors—veterans *and* newcomers. Who can resist potting up the enchanting little plantlets which appear on big leaves, to make *more* Piggybacks? Give them east or west light and a cool 65° and they multiply faster than guinea piggies!

The satisfying characteristic of simple plants like these is that they are adaptable; they fill a need for an uncomplicated expression. They should *not* be put down just because they are common. Enjoy. And then, when someone admires one of them, hand it over and say "It's yours!" Sharing plants is a special human exchange. It also justifies your buying another plant to take its place, with no feeling of guilt.

"Easies" give beginners reassurance that not every plant brought home is going to die (known as the Lament of Purple Thumbs). A taste of success is the beginning stage of becoming a plant parent—and a whole new attitude about trying not-so-easies. Anyone-can-grow-them plants lap up attention but don't sulk if it is not given. They are plants which are uncomplicated and "fit in."

Take the *Aloe,* a sturdy upright succulent with thick fleshy leaves and toothy edges. It sits happily in a warm dry room with moderate watering during the winter-spring months, can go years without repotting, and sends out a large cluster of bell-shaped flowers from early March into July. Or, look at Grape ivy, *Cissus rhombifolia,* a vigorous trailing green which lives placidly in places others can't tolerate (but subject to retarded growth—all plants respond to good light for normal growth); hang it in a stairwell, on top of the refrigerator, over a desk. German ivy, *Senecio mikanoides,* will survive short energy crises because it is one of the old "cast-iron" breed; the leaves are unaffected, thinner and shinier than those of Grape ivy. German ivy takes more water, more light.

59

ANYONE CAN GROW THEM

Still talking about ivies—but not necessarily true ivy—there's Creeping Charlie, or Swedish ivy, sprouting in windows from San Francisco to Newfoundland. I think C.C. and Piggyback must run stem-and-stem for national popularity. There are professional growers with as many as a million plants under cultivation, on their way to those windows! Meanwhile, each time *you* pinch back your Creeping Charlie, you'll find yourself making cuttings. Something's got to give.

Tahitian Bridal Veii is a gay deceiver because it looks so tender and delicate. Don't worry, it has durable Wandering Jew stamina in its stems. Just keep it out of hot sun and drafts.

To repeat, *don't* let anyone put you down for growing easies. Select plants which please your eye, your feelings, then get the adoption papers ready. Reverse snobbism is doing your thing at any level.

In addition to the plants described on the following pages, other easy-to-grow plants are: Asparagus fern, Chinese Evergreen, *Columnea,* Jade plant, Corn palm, *Maranta,* Spider plant and Wandering Jew.

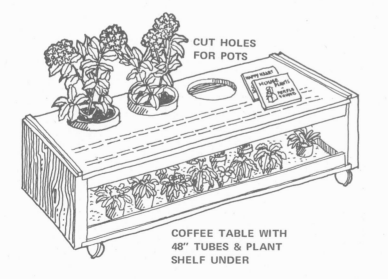

CUT HOLES
FOR POTS

COFFEE TABLE WITH
48" TUBES & PLANT
SHELF UNDER

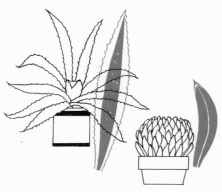

AGAVE

Later in this book you'll find Tree *Agave (A. attenuata),* a large decorator's standby for big space (see Plants Your Cat Won't Nibble). *Agave marginata* and *Agave victoriae reginae* are significant because they are manageable size, snap-of-the-finger easy.

Agave marginata is a small handsome yellow-margined cactus, trouble-free and sturdy, but not recommended if there are children in the family who might have a run-in with it.

Agave victoriae reginae, named for Queen Victoria, is a friendly little window plant, and may mature so slowly it can use that sill for 10 years before needing a new home. The leaves are thick, three-sided, and grow out of the trunkless center like an exploding artichoke. Olive green leaves have white edges and markings, and only if you are careless will pointy leaves bite you (margins are toothless).

Plant *Agave* in a cactus mix which you can buy; be sure the drainage works. For care, plan at least four hours of sun each day, dry air like that in an office, and watering on the wet-to-dry plan, with only enough in winter to keep it from withering. Feed once a year in spring.

Propagation: the Queen by seeds; *A. marginata* from young shoots growing at the base of the cactus.

BLUE GUM

Invite a tree to lunch today—if you wait 20 years it may be 50 feet too tall—particularly if you adopt the Blue Gum, *Eucalyptus globulus,* a real challenge to try and to enjoy. Even a couple of years ago no one would have thought of the Gums from Australia as housebroken because they take big space.

Why not try? Once Blue Gum outgrows you, give it to a park or plant it on a country lot; meanwhile you've had two or three years with a remarkable adolescent. Look for it at your nursery; select young trees with vigor and fullness. The price will be less than a modest pot of azaleas, and the size will give a room new scale.

When young, the Blue Gum's blue-green leaves are roundish, but as the tree grows they elongate and take on the familiar sickle shape. It is aromatic, that nose-tingling *Eucalyptus* fragrance. The flowers are creamy-white clusters.

The needs are simple: a large tub or half barrel, sun four hours a day, weekly feeding. It absorbs and transpires large amounts of water—don't let it dry out. Put it where the heat is lower in winter. Nip top shoots to force bushing, and repot, if you have to, in February. It tolerates warm dry rooms, is pest-free.

ANYONE CAN GROW THEM

BROMELIADS

This immigrant family from the primeval forests of Central and South America has made thousands of loyal Bromeliaddicts who can't resist getting more specimens even though they've run out of room.

Bromeliads are stemless perennials with fountain-spouting or vase-shape leaves, and are endowed with dramatic bloom. Many came out of tropic tree branches to settle in greenhouses and houses. All are decorative, and in the case of the pineapple, edible. And they take little expertise to grow.

Nourishment and water are taken in through the upper faces of the leaves, and the vase shape holds any moisture. Feed every two or three weeks; point the spout of your watering can right into the vase. Precaution: Rainwater or calcium-free water is their only dietary eccentricity. (I've found that tap water which doesn't clog a steam iron is okay.) Give as much light as possible, but not direct sun, and a good warm summer. If thermometer falls below 55°, you may find root rot and dark spots on the leaves.

Repotting is rarely called for but when you do it, use potting soil rich in leaf mold or peat. Feed the newly potted plant on a three-week schedule during spring and summer.

Propagation: from side shoots or rosettes taken from the plant after it has stopped flowering.

Guzmania monostachya: One of the larger bromeliads, has 20-inch funnel leaves in a rosette. Rounded tubular flower stems are covered with small red bracts and creamy tips; flowers themselves are white, red and dark brown, and last at least two weeks. Put it in diffused light (sun will burn), add warmth, high humidity and fast drainage.

Neoregilia spectabilis: Broad-leaf tongues with prickly edges; likes sun or bright light, high humidity, temperature. The leaves are exciting: ends are rich red so its nickname rates Painted Fingernail plant. The bloom in the center looks like smaller leaves but is bathed in red and blue and lasts for months. *Neoregilia* pots up in firbark or osmunda fiber.

Nidularium innocenti: Rosette of olive-green toothed leaves, black undersides. Copper or red bract in center forms a kind of nest where a white cluster hides (it's called Little Bird's Nest in the trade). Likes filtered light.

Tillandsia cyanea: Makes a stunning hanger because the narrow leaves swoop down below the bottom of the pot. Put several together to get a real fountain effect and the pleasure of many pink blossoms spouting on long stems, like the Spider plant.

Vriesia splendens: Coarse broad leaves with brown cross stripes in a large rosette. Flowering comes on a thick vertical sword spike which is red and lasts a long time. Small yellow flowers sneak out the sides.

GERMAN IVY

Also called Parlor ivy because, like the "cast-iron" plants, it survived erratic heat and care when nothing else would grow for the Victorians.

The thin, shiny, waxy leaves are simple, with shallower indents than English or Algerian ivy; new leaves are pale green. German ivies are friendly plants without any particular clout except their exuberant growth (to 20 feet in one year if you let them have their way).

Senecio mikanoides does furnish you with an easiest-to-care-for hanging plant where other angels fear to bed; they can be pruned and shaped and even taught to climb a wire topiary form. If the lower leaves shed, pot up cuttings (they root like water-babies) in the same container to close the gaps. Use several hanging in front of a window and you can dispense with blinds.

Moderate light, like a north opening, is excellent; winter sun is acceptable, but never in summer. This ivy is greedy for water yet can live in dry air. Inconspicuous yellow daisy-like flowers show up during winter.

Propagation: half-ripe wood cuttings, in water.

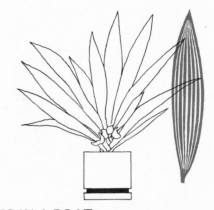

MOSES-IN-A-BOAT

If you turn to the cover of this book you'll see the *Rhoeo spathacea* in color, the purple rampant. This easy-to-adopt perennial is still another relative of Wandering Jew. They're happy-go-anywhere plants, sitting in unglazed ceramic holders (like the tree trunk druid) or baroque urns, or double-potted in a People's Republic of China rattan basket.

Leaves are lance-shape, up to a foot long, striped with yellow and green on top and red-purple under, bending and curving or erect. Funky little boats, perhaps an inch across, appear down among the leaves, and out pop dainty white stars, over and over again. When they reach the end of blooming, the neck below the boat turns brown, and you have a cargo of seeds ready to start several flotillas.

Rhoeo, also known as Moses-in-the-Cradle, takes high or moderate light from an east or west window, and a temperature range from 50° to 72°. Keep it barely moist but don't let it dry out completely. Likes a humid summer, a dry warm winter (leaves roll up in dry air; mist once in a while).

Pot up in packaged soil, with a handful of sand thrown in for good measure. Feed every two weeks until September, then let it rest until March.

Propagation: cuttings of side shoots, or seeds.

63

ANYONE CAN GROW THEM

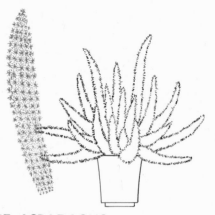

PINK POLKADOT

Also lovingly tagged Freckle Face. Two- to three-inch soft downy leaves peppered with pink spots identify Pink Polkadot, *Hypoestes sanguinolenta*. For some obvious reason, it has a kind of magnetism in a plant store, and shoppers are drawn to touch and to turn around a pot.

It's possible to encourage growth to two feet tall, but as a four- or six-inch pot, it has the charm of a young kitten. *Hypoestes* is a beginner's love, or a companion for a retired mailman, something pleasant to talk to. Its only personal problem is that it tends to get weedy, and should be pinched back with a firm parental hand; you'll want to force bottom growth anyway. Inconspicuous lilac blooms appear, but the leaves are its asset. Variety "Splash" has big dots.

Filtered light, humidity and bi-weekly feeding plus a constantly moist state—and you've got a friend for life (its life, that is).

Propagation: easy to buy—don't spend time waiting for seeds to grow.

PLUME ASPARAGUS

Big puffy plumes identify *Asparagus densiflorus meyerii*—hardly recognizable as relatives of the open airy *Asparagus sprengeri*. The plumes are fat with uncounted soft needles; stems range from one to two feet long, and six or sixteen can make a restful green cloud in the curtain-filtered bedroom light.

They can't stand sun—none of the *Asparagus* family can—but give them cool evenings down to 50° and daytime temperatures up to 75°, with frequent misting. Plume Asparagus should be potted in a good packaged soil which is always barely moist. Feed in March, in June and then in September. If it begins to look mangy, cut back and wait for new plumes.

Propagation: divide fleshy root clumps and cut back old plumes to let new growth develop. Also by cuttings and seeds.

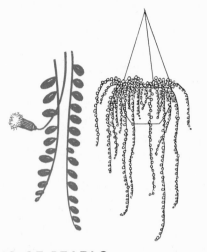

STRING OF PEARLS

One of nature's oddities: *Senecio rowleyanus* is a trailing succulent with quarter- to half-inch leaves shaped like beads—or even more like so many peas on a string. They're bright green, and the connector is a mere thread carrying food to each leaf. Some threads get six to eight feet long, so place the plant with this in mind. Hangers or pot holders on posts (see detail page 98) give you a clue. A clay pot of many strands, each a different length, makes an amusing captivator. The strands are delicate and take gentle handling: put the pot out of reach of pets and preschoolers, in bright light.

Senecio rowleyanus is another member of the *Senecio* family, which includes cinerarias and Dusty Miller as well as German ivy in this section, but one which changed its destiny to succulents.

Being succulent, String of Pearls is easy to raise and won't expire if left to dry out on occasion. Miniature daisy-like flowers appear at odd moments on the strands, and there's a faint scent of carnations as you pass by.

Propagation: broken strands.

SWEDISH IVY

Plectranthus australis also answers to the name Creeping Charlie. Because of its current popularity, it may just cover the earth like that paint company threatened years ago. Look in any window and you may recognize the familiar trailing shape, the red-tinged and scalloped sprawly leaves.

Swedish ivy is obviously a "hanger," but I like it on a pedestal or an old stool or on the corner of a kitchen spice shelf. It grows in medium or bright light. Don't overwater because too much makes the leaves lose their crisp touch and turn dark. Likes cool airy space, and extra peat in the soil mix for drainage. Bonus: tiny white flowers, faintly fragrant.

Creeping Jennie, or Moneywort *(Lysimachia nummularia),* is similar to Creeping Charlie, but has roundish pairs of leaves which are light green and have yellow blooms at the joints; takes same kind of upbringing.

P.S. Stems break easily—this may also account for the creeping that's going on!

Propagation: cuttings or end sections.

65

ANYONE CAN GROW THEM

TAHITIAN BRIDAL VEIL

Tripogandra multiflora is the dainty lady of the Wandering Jew tribe (it is also catalogued as *Tradescantia multiflora).* Olive-green leaves with purple overtones grow close together on thin stems. The whole family of Wandering Jews is identified by the nodes or marked spaces between pairs of leaves which give it another common name: Inch plant.

There is multi-branching and crisscrossing of the stems until they become a thicket which spills over the edge. So it too needs a hanging pot to show off its best. Then, in summer, there's a shower of delicate white flowers, that bridal veil magic.

Tripogandra must be protected from direct sun—bright or moderate light okay—and from cool rooms or blasts of wind from winter windows. Soil is best if moist but not soaking. A satisfactory potting medium is one part peat moss and two parts packaged soil. Pinch the ends of the stems (if you can sort them out!) to encourage that bouquet-fullness.

Propagation: cuttings can be rooted in water.

YUCCA

Perhaps you know it as Spanish Bayonet, of the prickly tips and great western movie profile. No John Wayne picture can be made without *Yucca* extras. It says "desert" as surely as a man and his "hoss" riding into the sunset.

Because its tough blue-green leaves can puncture more than an inflated conversation, keep the *Yucca* out of the line of traffic. A young one will measure 18 inches across and eventually develop a three-foot spread indoors when the plant is about 10 years old. The bloom finally appears then—a tall spike with a white cluster tinged with purple. Let your guests keep a respectful distance.

Yucca aloifolia is the bachelor's special: no special care, just a heavy dose of sunlight and moderate watering in summer, fading away to an almost dry November to February. Keep it cool in winter, and that's about all; except, avoid overwatering.

Yucca aloifolia variegata, the variegated form, has yellow to white markings.

Propagation: cut out offsets.

ACHIMENES

Q *Will my Achimenes bloom more than once?*

A This lovely gesneriad, with velvety pink, red, orange, blue-purple or white blooms which appear from June until October, is grown from rhizomes. Hold back on watering and let the plants cool down naturally. When it's winter rest time, remove the rhizomes and store them in dry sand or vermiculite until January or February when you replant, half a dozen to a good-sized pot. Cover the rhizomes with soil and keep them somewhat moist, and warm. Then you should get a repeat of blossoms. Furnish warmth, and bi-weekly feedings during bloom.

ALOE

Q *Do I have to do anything special to propagate an Aloe cutting?*

A Start with a sterilized knife and keep all the action clean so you won't introduce fungus diseases to the new stem cutting. Once the cutting is made, let it rest for a few days to callus the cut end, a self-healing process. If you're in a hurry, put the end against a hot iron, then dip in hormone powder, and plant.

ARROWHEAD PLANT

Q *I have been rooting an Arrowhead plant in water and it has lots of roots. When should I plant it?*

A *Syngonium,* or *Nephthytis,* is water-oriented; if you replace the water monthly, it will continue to be happy in its own pool. You can drop a few grains of gardener's charcoal into the container, some sand and some gravel to make it seem more special. Or, you can pot it up now into a dish garden or a terrarium, keeping it generally moist. Protect it from blasts of cold air and sudden temperature changes.

ASPARAGUS FERN

Q *Can I grow an Asparagus fern and a Boston in the same light?*

A Yes, even though Asparagus isn't a true fern. Keep both out of sunlight and keep the room on the cool side, between 55° and 65°; mist to discourage red spider. Bostons, Maidenhair and Bird's Nest take more misting, high humidity.

Q *What makes my Asparagus fronds turn yellow?*

A Inadequate light is one of the causes. Other reasons for yellowing could be too much or too little watering—ferns must have moisture but not sogginess, and excellent drainage. A sickly fern is an irritation; cut it back and hope for new life at the center.

BROMELIAD

Q *What causes a bromeliad to stand still and do nothing for months and months?*

A The tap water you give may be hard water, or water with softener added. Try catching rainwater or put the plant outside during a rain. You should be putting the water in that "vase" which the leaves form; the soil gets only moderate watering. Bromeliads are light feeders and like a misting of the food on their leaves.

CHINESE EVERGREEN

Q *I saw a huge pot of Chinese Evergreen. How is that done? I would like to try it.*

A *Aglaonema* needs very damp soil and can even be grown in water. I would guess the big plant is made up of many individual ones, and was grown in a warm north window, with a heavy hand on the watering can. Fertilizer doesn't make much difference in size, but humidity does.

ANYONE CAN GROW THEM

CHRYSANTHEMUM

Q *Will the mums I bought at my supermarket bloom again next year?*

A Enjoy what you bought now because your plants have been forced into bloom and aren't likely to have any more to give. If you have a garden, try planting them there and with luck you may get bloom the following year, but never like the original. This won't work in cold climate gardens because these plants are greenhouse born and raised and will not tolerate cold.

COLEUS

Q *I've had a Coleus for about six months and it looked great for a while but now the plant has too many branches and the leaves seem smaller.*

A Cut it back and make new cuttings. Spring is a good time to do this. This bushy plant is easy to grow so don't waste time on a tired sire: toss out the remnants of the old plant and start fresh. Give them good sun and regular waterings and feedings.

COLUMNEA

Q *My Columnea is stringy and its flowers very scarce. What's recommended for this?*

A *Columnea* needs warmth and a bright window. If the temperature drops below 60° at night it gets inhibited. Stand the pot on a moist pebble tray to increase humidity. Prune and pinch when the plant is young to get fullness. Make cuttings of the prunings and pot with the parent plant, if it's too late to change its habits.

CROTON

Q *What causes the leaves of the croton I brought from Hawaii to drop? There are only two left.*

A Croton is fussy about drafts and dryness. Up the humidity immediately, giving it misting several times a day and setting the pot on a moist-pebble saucer. Sunlight excites the color. If you have a garden, set the pot outside on warm days.

DIEFFENBACHIA

Q *The Dieffenbachia on my office desk looks terrible. Why are the leaves so dull and droopy?*

A Most office atmospheres are dry and the light is too limited. Find a better light, like a north window, and be sure the pot sits on a pebble-filled saucer partially filled with water to give the needed humidity. Mist the plant, particularly during hot weather. If it looks repulsive, take the plant home and cut it down to the soil line. It will come back again. You can cut the stem into three-inch lengths and propagate new plants by keeping them in warm moist sand.

DRACAENA

Q *My Dracaena has brown spots on the edges. Are these signs of bugs?*

A More likely they are sun scald from having been near a south window exposure.

Q *If the leaves on my Corn palm turn yellow, is there something I should feed it?*

A Check first to see if you find signs of red spider mite. Wash the leaves with a soapy solution, both top and bottom. In fact, keep the leaves free of dust to discourage any pest invasion. There may be an iron deficiency, but it's not likely in most *Dracaena*.

FLOWERING MAPLE

Q *The leaves of my Flowering Maple are getting brown and some of them are falling.*

A Too much sun and lack of moisture in the air can send *Abutilon* into a leaf-drop spin. The soil needs soaking in summer, with misting a couple of times a day. Cut the water back to barely moist in winter. Leaf-fall may also be the result of a spider mite invasion: Wash the plant in tepid water twice a week, and spray outdoors with an insecticide if the mites persist. Flowering Maple can stand cutting back or pinching when young to make it bushy; you can root the cuttings any time of the year.

GERMAN IVY

Q *I thought German ivy liked lots of sun; the leaves on mine shriveled.*

A Quick! move it to a cool spot, 50° to 60°, and keep it nicely moist. Take some healthy cuttings and start rooting them in water or moist sand. When they're ready to be planted, cut out the scorched parts of the parent plant and replace with cuttings.

GRAPE IVY

Q *You say Grape ivy is easy to grow; why doesn't mine put out new leaves?*

A *Cissus* needs constant moisture. Also, it will probably start new shoots if you give it more light. Move the vine to an east or west window for a couple of months and you'll see big growth.

Q *How often should I feed Grape ivy?*

A If you use liquid fertilizer, add about half a teaspoon to a quart of water, once a week from March through August. Begin to cut back on watering, and during November through February, no feedings.

SPIDER PLANT

Q *Why do the tips of my Spider plant turn brown?*

A If the plant is allowed to dry out too long, tips will brown; take a pair of sharp fingernail scissors to trim away, and the *Chlorophytum* will look almost as good as new. Some plants resent touching and handling and show their annoyance with browned tips.

SWEDISH IVY

Q *My Creeping Charlie has been on the fire escape and its leaves are small and reddish instead of large green. What happened?*

A One possibility: it may have got a chill; *Plectranthus* needs normal temperatures, moisture and humidity. Another possibility: It was allowed to dry out. One of the Swedish ivies has small leaves with a purple cast, and this may be a natural reason for the color of your plant.

UMBRELLA TREE

Q *Why does the soil under my Umbrella tree have some white stuff on it? Also, should the soil pull away from the sides of the pot?*

A First question: The white is usually caused by salts in the water you use or comes from excess fertilizer salts. Give the plant a thorough soaking by placing the pot in a pail of tepid water and let it stand at least an hour. Remove and let drain, and repeat; this will leach some of the excess salt. Also, in answer to the second question: The soaking will have solved the soil being pulled away from sides of pot. You have been underwatering—*not* that you should water oftener, but when you *do* water, give the *Schefflera* a thorough watering, then let it become almost dry before repeating. Dribs-and-drabs of water are less desirable than the method above.

PLANTS TO SUPPLANT FURNITURE

This section is dedicated to anyone who has a personal repotting coming up. If you are faced with a move, this may just be the shift where you turn over an old leaf. New beginnings are opportunities to go in fresh directions. Change your living patterns, rearrange belongings, shed parts which bore.

Consider what happens when a plant is repotted: You're doing the too-tight roots a big favor by giving them more space; you're encouraging growth. Pruning and shaping are parts of repotting, too. That's what we all face when it's time to ferry possessions from one place to another. That's why people have garage sales, and Goodwill Industries thrives. Getting rid of unused pasts softens the frustration of *where will I put what is here . . . in there?* Before you start assigning furniture to new floor and wall spaces, think *change*. What would happen if . . . .

Go look at the new spaces with a seeing eye: the empty apartment, the unfinished tract house, the sterile condominium. Have you stood in this naked room and really looked at it—with not a stitch of furniture on, nothing but bare nails in walls where others' pictures left only dusty traces—where you will live?

For instance, what if you moved in nothing but one enormous house plant, something bigger than you've ever experienced? What happens to that room is that it is clothed. Suddenly, the room needs less furniture. Subtly, you feel *change*. A Chinese Fan palm, with its three-foot leaves, left planted in its metal container but then set in a gigantic basket, can bring more environmental impact into the space than if Euell G. himself came to dinner.

A multi-stem six-foot *Schefflera* or a sturdy *Tupidanthus* in its own clay pot, double-potted in a rectangular flue tile which has been placed on a roll-around dolly, becomes the Tree of Hope for an unending remodel of an older house. (I remember wiping sawdust off *Schefflera* leaves every week for a whole year.)

A bay window can be furnished no more eloquently than with a great dark green *Acanthus* in a wood tub; put the tub on casters so you

PLANTS TO SUPPLANT FURNITURE

can chase dustballs underneath—and move the whole shebang outside on a summer's day.

Hide a hideous fireplace, with its phony gas logs: Plant a Snowflake tree in half an olive barrel. Before planting, refinish the barrel with sanding and varnishing and lacquer the metal straps black. Line the inside with a non-toxic mastic sealer; be sure the container has drainage holes and a saucer underneath to catch the water.

Search out an old copper laundry-boiling kettle in a countryside secondhand store. Burnish the metal and touch up the wooden handles. Add a Castor Oil tree or a Rice Paper plant (see Plants to Back Up Other Plants).

Set a great cactus on top of an old butcher's block. Put a tree next to a stairwell and hook up light to give it stardom. There's no doubt about it: big plants supplant furniture . . . in the nicest ways! Are *you* ready for the big change?

In addition to the plants described on the following pages, other plants to supplant furniture are: the giant cacti: *Pachypodium, Cryptocereus* (huge hanging type), *Echinocactus* (up to three feet in diameter); palms; tree ferns; *Monstera deliciosa;* bamboo.

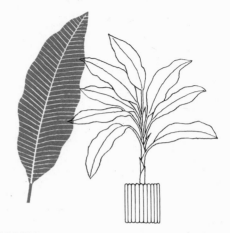

BEAR'S BREECH

Subtract one tired pseudo-Victorian sofa with bear-claw feet—and substitute one magnificent Bear's Breech with its two- to three-foot leaves. Throw a couple of jumbo pillows on the floor. One thing is sure, you'll never forget *that* room as long as you live.

Acanthus mollis has always been an outside accent plant. Who would have thought it could come indoors and make its living so simply? It seems that all it takes is partial sun, a little extra sand in the soil when you repot to inspire better drainage (it's a heavy drinker), and mild feeding once a month. You might throw in a leaf-washing or misting in summer to make it grunt happily.

Bear's Breech grows from rhizomes, so there is no central trunk—just this commune of huge and glistening dark green leaves. There can be a striking flower spike, white or purple, but you'll have to furnish more sun. However, if size of leaves is your room's thing, cut the blossom to insure more leaf growth.

Propagation: division of rhizomes spring or fall.

BANANA

Bold fast-growing trees—not the dwarf varieties, but big specimens with 24-inch leaf blades and five feet of growth. Banana, *Musa nana cavendishii*, becomes tall sculpture, a logical contender for a two-story opening, an 11-foot ceiling or an indoor bath garden. Without further decoration, the decorating is done. *Musa* will spread sideways as it grows, but if the light is overhead, leaves will reach up for it.

The only hitch is too-dry air on a warm day; you'll need some kind of ventilation to reassure the banana, to step up the humidity. Otherwise, all it needs to flourish is acid soil, moist summers and drier winters. Good feeding every two weeks and an occasional dusting of the leaves helps too. There is no assurance of a bunch of fruit one morning for your pet primate, but who needs it when one can go bananas over a piece of living furniture!

If you have an outdoors, a balcony, patio or garden, move the tubbed *Musa* out in summer. Don't let it dry out because the soil must always be damp but not soggy. Banana should get the brightest light possible but not direct summer sun which will sunburn leaves. Maximum winter sun is ideal.

Propagation: seeds (very slow), or repot suckers with roots attached.

73

PLANTS TO SUPPLANT FURNITURE

CHINESE FAN PALM

Move out the Steinway! This imposing palm has the largest leaves of any palm which will grow indoors; Fan palms in Southern California gardens can easily bear seven-foot wide fronds. However, I doubt if you will have to move out: *Livistona chinensis* are available as young plants 12 to 18 inches tall, and they are not fast growers.

It's just that middle-age spread comes (as it does to all) and you'll find yourself supporting a palm with three- to four-foot leaves after a few years. The leaves, made up of many fingers, are cut only to the middle and tend to bend there with all points toward the floor. Thread fibers hang between the fingers, and spines parade down the lower part of the stalk.

Livistona is no chore to adopt; the plant throws off its unwanted dead leaves. When you repot, use a soil rich in leaf mold; add sand and planter's charcoal to sweeten the needed constantly moist condition. Likes cooler nights than days, about 60°, and fog or mist will be appreciated. Fertilize in March and September, but wait six months before feeding a newly potted palm. Watch for red spider mites and scale; take palm outdoors, wash with soapy suds and rinse. Try a systemic treatment for scale in addition to the sudsy bath.

ELEPHANT'S EAR

Big is not necessarily best, but certainly the Elephant's Ear is one of the easier *Philodendron* to grow, and *Philodendron* species are safe answers to any interior. Given both reasons, plus the modest price of a big Ear compared to a piece of furniture you yearn for but can't swing now, there could scarcely be a better stand-in. *Philodendron hastatum* was one of the first investments made in our studio during remodeling, and it thrived in five different locations, playing musical chairs with a table saw.

Hastatum has a 12- to 18-inch long arrow leaf with red-veined underside. The calla-like flower in its advanced age has a strong perfume, opens at the unlikely time of three a.m. and lasts for a while. It's a vining type of plant and can use a stout bamboo stake to lean on, or a tall wood post wrapped with moist moss or sphagnum.

Philodendron wendlandii is "self-heading" instead of vining, and has huge 18-inch leaves. *P. selloum* has 20- to 30-inch ones with deeply cut edges.

They all like good potting mix, good light (no sun), and will show leaf spot if too moist or warm. Water on a regular soaking-to-dry cycle, and feed once a month, spring to fall.

Propagation: cuttings, in water.

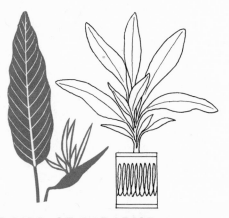

GIANT BIRD OF PARADISE

This is a temporary furniture diversion: by the time the two- to three-foot leaves take over, you should consider evicting the plant and rethink the space. But at least three years of indoor fascination are in store for the owner of a *Strelitzia reginae.* It is not usually found in a plant boutique, so try your nurseryman. Ask for five-gallon containers and pot up in a wooden tub.

This five-foot relative of the banana is trunkless and has compact blue-gray leaves and an exotic flowering which emerges from the top of a long stiff stem. The blossom pops out of a boat-shaped bract, has a red and orange bill and a bright blue tongue. *Strelitzia augusta* has a white blossom, and *S. nicolai* grows to 15 feet, with reddish bracts cradling white flowers and blue tongue.

It's a tough plant, loves sun and takes a widespread temperature from 72° down to 50° in winter. Water on a wet-to-dry cycle; add liquid fertilizer twice a month from April through August. These birds will take up to 10 years from seed to bloom, so in order to get the exciting blossom, you're smart to start with a large specimen. It can be put in a mild-climate garden later, or gifted to friends with a taller ceiling.

SNOWFLAKE TREE

Okay. This will be a hard one to find. Ask a local garden center or the biggest nursery in the county to locate a *Trevesia palmata*—and you'll be able to forego the $1500 armoire you covet, the chandelier with real candles. Once you've seen a Snowflake tree, *there* will be the interior decoration for any room.

The wildly lobed leaves are perhaps 24 inches across, with edges cut by some giant's pinking shears, and held together with webs like a duck's foot. The ribs are pale, prominent, the stems brown and prickled. Showy—and beautiful. If you are really lucky, superb white flowers may appear. It can grow to 15 feet tall, but will probably stay room-locked with temperate attention.

Trevesia is a dues-paying member of the *Aralia* tribe; that calls for increased humidity, moist soil, and no direct sunlight. The very much simpler *Aralia, Dizygotheca elegantissima,* wants a soilless mixture, warmth (never below 60°) and normal watering with a little less in winter. Never feed a dry root ball but moisten first and add nourishment twice a month.

PLANTS TO SUPPLANT FURNITURE

BANANA TREE

Q *I inherited a large tubbed banana tree. What time of the year will it start having fruit?*

A That depends on variety and if the *Musa* is contented with its warmth and moisture. Usually they won't produce unless there is 30 to 40 percent humidity and you give the tree a good misting every day. In the middle of the day, be sure it gets bright light but no sun when it's hot. Never let a banana dry out, and if you can roll the plant outside in shade during summer, it will be an encouragement. Watch for spider mites.

PHILODENDRON

Q *I cut back my Split-Leaf Philodendron. The leaves on the cutting are not splitting or getting holes. Why is nothing happening?*

A This is a genetic failing of the *Philodendron* family. The first few leaves revert to the original simple leaf form, but as the cutting gets older, it will finally develop and you will be rewarded. Starting the cutting in water gives it less nourishment and a less vigorous start, so the split leaves may take even longer to appear. On an older plant, if the soil is tired or needs more nourishment at the roots, leaves will sometimes rebel and not split.

AERIAL ROOTS

Q *Can I cut off the aerial roots of my Philodendron?*

A The *Philodendron* family is generally a vining type (there are several self-heading ones which need no support). The aerial roots attach themselves to the tree against which the vine is growing. These roots also get moisture and nutrients from the host. Indoor *Philodendron* don't need the roots, and I have periodically cut them off without any damage. Some experts insist that the roots be trained into the vine's container, so if you want to compromise, clip a few, plant a few.

MOVING PLANTS

Q *Even if I found a huge plant to bring into my apartment, how do I get it in? Also, big pots are terribly expensive. I can't afford both pot and plant.*

A A big plant weighs less than a piano, is actually more flexible and you'll find movers handle plants today with awareness and care. If you have to cut corners, a friend's station wagon and two husky males can maneuver almost anything which will fit an apartment. A tall specimen plant can be laid on its side, with a soft blanket underneath, and wedges set on both sides of the pot to keep it from rolling when the car corners. Protect the exposed leaves from wind whipping with a tarp or sheet plastic. Use a child's wagon or a rented dolly for the short runs on flat surfaces. An old drop cloth or burlap under the container helps slide large pots across floors indoors. Baskets are cheaper than pots and come in a great range of sizes. Put a large saucer inside the basket and set the container on it. Fill the space between pot and basket with sphagnum moss. If the budget won't buy a basket, use a plastic garbage can; you can cover it with rejection slips, canned food labels or anything funky which fits your style. Wood boxes used as shipping cases can often be had for the asking; stain the box and put wood strips underneath to lift the box off the floor. Simple wood boxes can be made of old barn siding, or leftover redwood decking.

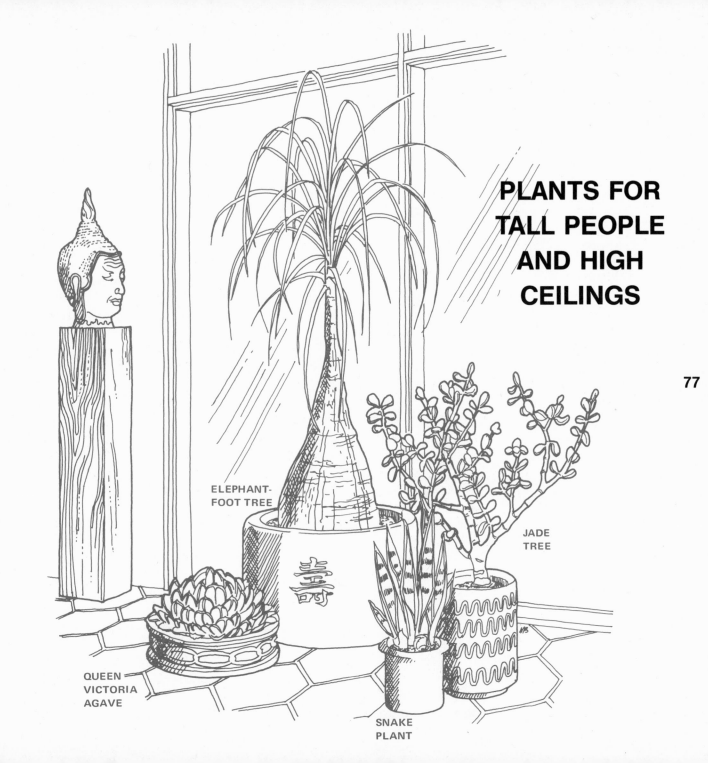

**PLANTS FOR
TALL PEOPLE
AND HIGH
CEILINGS**

ELEPHANT-
FOOT TREE

JADE
TREE

QUEEN
VICTORIA
AGAVE

SNAKE
PLANT

PLANTS FOR HIGH CEILINGS

The unabridged dictionary lists 43 definitions of the word "scale." But only one fits today's connotation of architects and planners, painters and sculptors who measure an intangible relationship between a space and what fits in that space. Most of us are unconscious of why we feel certain things about the spaces we live in—too big, too small, too crowded—or the reverse: Are they lonely, empty?

What I'm trying to say is that the plants you select for a room which is taller than standard eight-foot height should have scale relating to that extra space up there. A dozen bitsy pots on the floor of a room with a 10-foot ceiling will be lost, like a seed-pearl necklace on the bosom of Mae West. Big rooms demand big thinking. Just as tall people require longer slacks, a high ceiling needs at least one important tree—or several plants at different heights, all grouped together, to make the scale impressive—and make it relate to the people who live there.

For the lucky few who have contemporary glass walls and high ceilings, an olive tree in a big tub indoors will never cease to stamp its indelible feeling on your pleasure. *Olea europaea* needs year-round south sun exposure and ventilation to keep the heat range between 70° and 50°, and a couple of spring-summer feedings each year. Keep it pruned so that, if you have to move it out someday, you won't be like the boat builder with the too-small basement door. Try *Osmanthus fragrans*, Sweet Olive, with its jasminy bloom, if you can't hack a real olive; it will reach six feet indoors, bushing more and demanding less sun. Planted in a big oriental ceramic bowl, it is fit company for oversize rooms and people.

If you're dealing with a forbidding entrance hall, move in a couple of Grecian laurels, add strings of tiny white lights and put small pots of bloom right on top of the soil when it's party time—no one will notice the cobwebs up the stairs.

Even with inflation, it's still possible to buy large plants from a nursery, plants normally found in the garden. You'll get a negative attitude from the nurseryman about your chances of indoor success. But, for the price of a pair of theatre tickets you can get a *Pittosporum tobira* perhaps six feet tall—and even if you only keep it alive one year, compare the difference against one night's entertainment. Meanwhile, you've accepted challenge and given a good room a great break.

Take chances. Just follow a few rules for acclimating and you've increased the tree's chances a hundred percent: Start first at a top-drawer nursery, and start looking in spring, after the frost is off the pump. Beware of bugs and bum shapes; look for healthy trees with hefty trunks and pleasant branch arrangements. If there are roots sneaking out the bottom of the container it may be root bound; when feeder roots are pinched, the plant may never get off the ground.

Once it is bought and delivered, give your tree a refreshing shower to perk it up and to wash off any stowaway pests. Then give it a hefty drink of tepid water to leach out accumulated fertilizer salts, and let it drain well. Prune out any broken branch tips, and pinch back some of the new growth, just to get it interested in bushing out once it moves indoors. Keep an eye on leaves and stems after it is finally placed to be sure nothing serious is hatching.

In addition to the plants described on the following pages, other plants for tall folk and high ceilings are: *Aucuba,* Fiddle Leaf fig, Jade tree, Japanese maple, *Monstera deliciosa,* any of the palms and tree ferns, *Podocarpus, Schefflera,* Weeping fig.

LADY
PALM

79

WOOD
EDGE

BRICK OR TILE PAD TO
PROTECT FLOOR, LINE
WITH POLYETHYLENE

PLANTS FOR HIGH CEILINGS

BAMBOO PALM

Yet another tall palm, this one has multiple reed-like trunks like the bamboo clan, but fronds which identify a true palm. Bamboo palm, *Chamaedorea seifritzii,* grows stiff and vertical like the Parlor palm *(Chamaedorea adenopodus)* with its fat goldfish-tail leaves (see Plants for Skinny Places). Bamboo palm's leaves are quite delicate, pinnate; that is, they are long thin fingers. Unlike other palms, they do not all arch in the same direction. Each seems to take its own tack, so there's a relaxed attitude to counteract the rigid verticality of the slim trunk. Stems and stalks are more orange than green, another thing which sets the palm apart.

Bamboo is a hardy number, wanting only thorough watering and then to be left alone until almost dry. Leaves bleach out in sun exposure, so confine to an area of bright light and ventilation. No need to look for a cool winter spot: this one doesn't mind warmth. Give it weekly spring and summer feeding.

Shop for a Bamboo palm on its way to being a six- or seven-footer. You won't have to repot for years.

Propagation: seeds, very slow to grow.

COFFEE TREE

My favorite Italian coffee house in San Francisco's North Beach is Graffeo's. Along with a marvelous pungent burnt bean fragrance, there's a 10-foot Coffee tree in an east window right next to the churning roaster. It's healthy, happy, and has descendants from cuttings all over the city.

Coffee arabica trees reach 10 to 12 feet indoors. The dark glossy form is vertical, evergreen. Leaves are thin but firm and wavy, and tips often are curled. Give it bright light in summer, a south or west one from September to April, always shading the roots. One day you'll be rewarded with some pure white blossoms with a delicate fragrance. After the blossoms, you just might, if you're lucky, get red cherry-like drupes, or fruit, with woody shell and two beans inside each one . . . after six months of waiting. Oh, well—it was a nice idea.

About watering: keep it barely moist but never soggy. Average temperatures, mist for humidity. Pinch back to increase bushiness, and fertilize every other week during growing season.

Look for a tall plant to fall in love with.

80

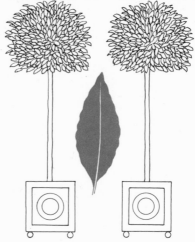

ELEPHANT-FOOT TREE

Beaucarnea recurvata is strictly for blithe spirits! Though its other common names are Bottle palm and Ponytail, it isn't a palm, it's not a pony—but it *is* an enchanting and amusing plant form. There is a strange swollen base, like a giant's wrinkled onion, and out of the top slender-branched, curving leaves plummet.

Set your sights for a really big one. Pass by the two-footers which are fairly easy to find, and shoot the budget on a rare six-footer with leaves from three to five feet long.

The remarkable base is a watertank; Elephant-Foot is a succulent from the deserts of Texas and Mexico. Indoors, you will want to give it a thorough watering and then let it dry out before repeating. Misting during extra-warm days advised. Try for 55° nights, 72° days. Feed once a year, in spring. *Beaucarnea* prefers a small container and is a slow grower. Good drainage essential. The plant dotes on sun but keep it away from hot window glass. Repotting is rare.

GRECIAN LAUREL

Enter, the formal tree. *Laurus nobilis,* source of leaves used in victory crowns for heroes and nobility in ancient Greece—and of bay leaves for seasoning the lowly pot roast. Laurel is a cool customer, needing only bright light like four hours of sun in summer and as much winter sun as possible. It is tolerant of less light, and doesn't complain of drafts.

The tall laurels will come from a nursery. To stay alive, they have to be acclimated; let them stand outside in light conditions similar to the nursery's. Water only enough to keep them from wilting, but do mist with the hose. Gradually move them to a more shaded position and give more water. Leaves may drop—that's normal for the move. Bring the trees indoors in September to a spot where there's bright light, and you should have it made. Feed monthly the following April to August with half-strength high nitrogen fertilizer. Keep soil barely moist—too much water gives leaves a jaundice complex.

Propagation: cuttings.

81

PLANTS FOR HIGH CEILINGS

JACARANDA

Jacaranda acutifolia is a romantic semi-evergreen tree from Brazil and Peru, with a ferny foliage and silky-violet clusters which appear between April and September. A very special tree for a place which calls for a special something.

Leaves are similar to those of the Mimosa, finely cut and arching. Blossom clusters are made up of two-inch tubes, in violet to lavender-blue. The white-blossomed variety is rare, longer blooming.

It adores greenhouse conditions, with high humidity, excellent ventilation. So even if you have to give up your trip to Iran, consider closing in a balcony with a polyethylene wall, or add a glass room to the kitchen, and immerse yourself in the green scene . . . let the *Jacaranda* be the queen scene. (Looking down from a second-story vantage point gives it even more visual impact.)

Jacaranda likes bright light but not sun indoors. Steady but not frequent watering is right; too little stunts its growth. Potting soil needs addition of sand.

Propagation: cuttings from half-ripened wood.

MOCK ORANGE

Mock Orange, *Pittosporum tobira,* is a common enough garden regular, but did you know it makes a handsome big indoor plant up to 10 feet tall? Basically it is a shrub; it can be pruned and shaped into a quixotic irregular sculpture standing alone, or be used as the axis for your major plant collection.

Mock Orange normally grows broad and dense, more shrub than tree. The waxy, rounded-tip leaves grow in rosettes, and in early spring white flowers with the fragrance of orange blossoms cover the *Pittosporum.* Round green fruit follows in the fall, filled with orange seeds (neither for eating).

A nursery is the logical place to find a large specimen. You'll have to acclimate it before moving it indoors; give it a few weeks in the garden or on a balcony, with restricted watering, feeding and less sunlight. Then move it into a brightly lighted area like a porch and let it adjust before you start pruning. Add acid fertilizer twice a year. Top-dress yearly in between three- to five-year repottings. Mist in hot weather; water on a moist-to-almost-dry cycle.

Propagation: cuttings, seeds.

OREGON GRAPE

Mahonia lomariifolia is grown for its silhouette: a sophisticated vertical plant which grows 10 to 12 feet tall, and rated P.G. (parental guidance) because of the long curving stems, each with 20 prickly leaves in a double row. It's simply not a plant for small children-oriented houses, or for entry ways where it can reach out and impale a passing guest. *Mahonia* is a looking-at statuesque tree, a great shadow-maker; and on Christmas day there will be a sunny crown of yellow blossoms which eventually turn into berries.

Oregon Grape is a nursery-grown plant which can be brought straight into the house if you share a cool, bright location. Direct sun, except very early morning and winter time, is out. Acid soil needed, like the Mock Orange, with addition of leaf mold and some agricultural charcoal. Cool 50° nights and 65° days are friendly, and if you feed monthly from April to August, it will provide a stunning green feature. Caution: Don't fertilize a newly potted one for six months.

Propagation: cuttings, seeds.

OSMANTHUS

The variegated *Osmanthus* has a holly-like leaf, white edged, neat and small. The shrub itself is a full-bodied shape, can be pruned and nipped and cajoled into an espalier or a tall slim tree, or just allowed to grow naturally to its maximum indoor height. You may not find it exciting, but there's something very friendly about the crisp green foliage and its white markings. And coming from a nursery it will probably be just ducky for limited petty cash.

Osmanthus heterophyllus 'variegatus' is a hardy, no-trouble-with-my-child plant. It will take cold blasts and occasional neglect without visible complaint; it can do with reflected light, leaving space for sun-bunnies. And it acclimates from its outdoor upbringing very obligingly.

Osmanthus fragrans, with larger glossy leaves, is broad and dense, and has heady white flowers with a fruity fragrance. Takes shade, or sun from the east.

Give *Osmanthus* good drainage, cool nights, minimal feeding. Pinch growing tips to encourage fullness.

Propagation: cuttings, in spring.

83

PLANTS FOR HIGH CEILINGS

SILK OAK

This tree appeared in *House Plants for the Purple Thumb* but is so programmed for tall spaces that it has to be repeated here. *Grevillea robusta* is a lacy tree with warm silver-green fernlike leaves on undulating branches—a tree to set a mood, to stir imaginative shadows, to plant at an entrance or fill a bedroom corner.

Silk Oak prefers a cool bright location (leaves go brown in direct sunlight) and moderate watering all year round. Too much water or extreme drought are its mortal enemies; roots suffer and show their resentment. Temperature should stay above 60°, and although dry air is okay, a good misting helps on hot days. It grows rapidly, gracefully. When young it has a Christmas tree shape, but broadens in the right places to grow old gracefully. Plan your budget for a big specimen so you get full impact of its beauty.

Don't go into shock if there's a leaf-fall in spring; this is a quirk of Silk Oak. Also, watch for spider mites, mealy.

Propagation: seeds (may grow three feet in a year).

TEXAS PRIVET

Ligustrum japonicum 'Texanum' is the blue-collar house plant among all the exotics and privileged. It's local-shrub-makes-good-without-having-traveled-from-Madagascar. It is familiar, hardy, not expensive. It takes drafts, temporary chills, dry hot air and easy care. Yet you can have a space-maker tree that grows up to 12 feet and transforms any ordinary sun spot into a garden terrace. Texas Privet has good posture and lustrous leaves. In spring many white blossoms appear (which may or may not turn into blue berries). Two or three Privets in a garden room become a green screen to filter lovely shadows.

Privet requires at least four hours of sun or very bright conditions. Water by soaking, then wait until it is barely moist before repeating; also, it's a heavy eater so add a tiny amount of plant food each time you water, from April through August. Repotting is a springtime job. Add sand for drainage. Mist weekly in winter; 40° to 65° is a good warmth range.

Propagation: cuttings, seeds.

COFFEE

Q *I cut the side shoots of a Coffee tree because I wanted to start some for friends. Doesn't cutting back encourage more growth?*

A Unfortunately, Coffee is one plant you seldom pinch back on the sides; top pruning, yes. Young plants grow in a skinny single trunk (that's why I plant at least three together in a pot to give a fuller form), and it's only as they get several years old that they begin branching sideways.

ELEPHANT-FOOT

Q *When do I transplant my Beaucarnea?*

A Only when there seems to be no more room for that big wrinkly base. It likes to be crowded, but when you can't stand the fact that it looks like it should be potted, just remember not to fit too big a shoe on the Elephant's foot. Best conditions are a mixture of one part each peat, loam and sharp sand, a half-tablespoon of superphosphate for each gallon of mixture and same quantity of high-phosphorus fertilizer. Withhold feeding until the following spring.

Q *Can Elephant-Foot take full sun?*

A Hopefully at least four hours a day. It survives with bright light but that sun bath is its best ally.

GOLD DUST

Q *I thought Gold Dust plant was a small shrub for outdoors.*

A In California *Aucuba* grows six to ten feet tall, I've seen 14-footers. I would say that with cool temperatures, 60° or less, you could expect tall results, which means this would make a porch or deck plant. Give lots of water and shade.

JACARANDA

Q *The leaves of my Jacaranda have been falling and I'm afraid I've done something to it.*

A If it is late winter, this is a natural defoliating time. I wouldn't worry as long as it gets sun and warmth, and moisture. Too much of the last and it will get lots of undesirable tender loose growth.

JADE PLANT

Q *I've seen Jade plants just covered with blossoms, but mine never has any. What should I do?*

A Flowers can be counted on when grown outdoors with some overhead protection from the sun. The tiny star-shape pink bloom should appear anytime between November and April. If there's chance of winter freeze, bring the *Crassula argentea* indoors because it can't take cold. Mine is 25 years old and I feel its great old tree form is more important to save than being concerned with blossoms. Young cuttings sometimes will bloom in spring if pot bound.

JAPANESE MAPLE

Q *Is Japanese maple the same as Flowering Maple?*

A No. The leaf form and open branching are very similar, but there the Japanese connection ends. *Acer palmatum* is the tree form, a true Japanese maple. Flowering Maple, *Abutilon,* is a South American vining shrub. Japanese maple likes a cool room and filtered sunlight. Water it well during the growing season, and then let it get almost dry before you repeat. Feed only every other month to keep it from outgrowing its place in the house.

PLANTS FOR HIGH CEILINGS

MOCK ORANGE

Q *I tried growing Mock Orange indoors but it died.*

A *Pittosporum tobira* is a garden shrub which is happiest left in the garden. But if you keep the temperature down indoors and give it cooled sunlight, it should live for a long and healthy life. Water it well when it feels dry. Also, it likes an acid soil.

OLIVE

Q *I loved the olive trees when I visited Greece. Could I try growing one indoors?*

A Yes, you may very well try and succeed. If you can find one at your nursery, it will take a short period of getting it used to the limits of house-living. Keep the plant in the nursery can in a sunny spot for a couple of weeks before repotting; add water only to keep it alive, but mist the leaves. Repot in a container that is big and deep, adding extra sand and a tablespoon of ground limestone per gallon of the potting mixture. Be sure the container has good drainage and is properly crocked. Move the newly potted plant to partial shade and watch the leaves for any sign of droop; if this happens, give it more sun again and proceed slowly. It should end up in full shade, preferably until fall, and then be moved indoors in filtered sun. It needs cool nights, and eventually year-round sun and ventilation to keep going. Mist when the temperature goes up. Olives have fragrant white flowers outdoors, but unless there is the needed sun, they may not decide to come out in the house.

SWEET OLIVE

Q *Is Sweet Olive the same as an olive?*

A No. It's another case where common names mislead. As plants they are often planted for the same effect, but *Osmanthus* will be an easier plant to keep alive in the house than common olive, *Olea europaea*. *Osmanthus* likes a cool room; common olive needs sun to survive, and cool nights.

WEEPING FIG

Q *What would cause the leaves of my Weeping fig to look dull and slightly speckled?*

A Sounds like you have an invasion of thrips on your *Ficus benjamina*. These are minute insects which scrape the underside of leaves. Finally they leave papery scars and make the tips curl up. Try a tepid spray of soapy water (mix a tablespoon of Ivory soap powder into a quart of water and apply it from a laundry mister). A solution of Malathion diluted according to bottle directions and sprayed on the undersides of the leaves once a week for three weeks would be the last-ditch cure. Do this outdoors. *Aralia*, avocado, *Asparagus* ferns and *Citrus* are potential thrips' victims.

PLANTS TO TRANSFORM DULL DINING ROOMS

COFFEE TREE

VELVET PLANT

GLASS SHELVES

BEGONIA

WAX VINE

HERBS ON A LAZY SUSAN

HINGED LATTICE SCREENS

ORIGINAL SILL OF WINDOW

DINING TABLE PUSHED AGAINST WALL

LEOPARD PLANT

LENGTHEN WINDOWS TO FLOOR

BRICK PAVING, WOOD EDGE

PLANTS FOR DULL DINING ROOMS

If you are lucky enough to have a real dining room—a room which has its own identity and not just an alcove or a table and four chairs at one end of the living room—you *are* lucky. Designers and builders cut that space out of plans when budgets are tight, as if it weren't important. It *is*—not just as a place to seat guests, but as a place for family reunions and even that newfangled idea, communicating.

Maybe those designers and builders acted because this room is half-used—twice, perhaps three times a day there's traffic. Less design thought is given to the dining area than any other place in a house or apartment for that reason. Yet, quite by non-planning, it becomes the one room which might be transformed into a plant island. This could charm teenagers into sitting through a meal with the family instead of "I've got to leave in six minutes, Mom"; or lure a husband into lingering over a second cup of tea and talk after supper. The planted room should make after-dinner small talk long and important.

Because a dining-room arrangement is established by furniture shape and location, the plant scene can be relaxed or formal: a massing of plants or one palm, a bay window flooded with hanging baskets in bloom, or a half a dozen herbs double-potted in a clutch of mugs on a lazy Susan in the center of the table.

Before you bring in the green, study the room. Do you feel the need of more space? Try pushing the table against a wall, preferably opposite a window. When there's a crowd to feed, pull it back to front and center. Meanwhile you've achieved a new open space—room to look at plants in front of the window, room to walk side by side instead of Indian file past the table, and even room for an inviting rocker.

A room with a mirrored wall doubles the size. Builders' supply centers sometimes have modestly priced 12-inch squares of mirror which can be attached by the do-it-yourself method. Or, try changing color at one end of a long narrow area. Wallpaper a blank wall with a photo mural of trees or a meadow—mail-order houses advertise these send-away-for scenes. Is there room for a garden-inspired lattice made of narrow lath by the resident carpenter?

Should the window or windows screen out a too-close neighbor? Add a series of glass shelves in front of the pane, and go on safari to collect rare African violets. Read through the color-leaf suggestions in this section and come up with a fascinating red-purple collection instead of green: *Iresine,* Jewel orchid, Purple Heart, Velvet plant.

Need more light? There are half a dozen ways to use the new fluorescent plant lights near windows, under shelves, which will benefit plants *and* you. Or, outside the window, paint a roof overhang white to reflect more light inside.

Do you have a bay window? Build a continuous shelf at sill level and display pots brought in for bloom from the garden. Lifting plants off the floor gives them proper emphasis. Collecting them in one area gives them growth insurance—plants live better together.

Put large plants on roll-around dollies. Set an aquarium-turned-terrarium on a parsons' table so it can be maneuvered. Turn a tea-trolley into a home for wayward Angel-Wing begonias. Convert an unused fireplace into a plant display case for a family of ferns by the addition of a grow-light up next to the flue. Take the doors off an old buffet and do the same thing—remembering to mist the green to keep them happy. Fill an old reed fernery with Ti plants interspersed with trailing Purple Heart, that Wandering Jew with its neat little orchid-color blossoms.

In addition to the plants described on the following pages, other plants to transform dull dining rooms are: *Caladium, Gloxinia,* geraniums, *Kalanchoe,* orchids, poinsettia, miniature roses, tuberous begonias.

PLANTS FOR DULL DINING ROOMS

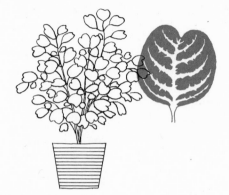

ANGEL-WING BEGONIA

Someone else coined the phrase "Begoniacs" for thousands of begonia collectors whose interest innocently started from a single plant and continues with hundreds. I'm warning this because it's easy to stray down the begonia path once you've tasted success.

The fibrous-rooted *Begonia semperflorens* are the seductive ones which will make you a Begoniaddict: Angel-Wings are tall perennials with distinguishing lopsided and patterned leaves—which may or may not resemble the celestial wing pattern, but whose colors are heavenly. Leaves and spectacular flowers hang out near the top of three-foot stems on mature plants; blossoms droop in clusters of white, pink or salmon and leaves are mottled silver, pink and bronze. Cane stems with wide-spaced joints are a distinctive characteristic of this easy to grow begonia.

Filtered sunlight and a barely damp but very porous soil are the only requisites. A good potting mixture of packaged potting soil and fine firbark, with added peat for a better acid balance, gives water retention yet essential drainage. Fertilize every other week with high-nitrogen food.

Propagation: stem cuttings.

BLOODLEAF

Try a fresh arrangement on a serving cart in the quiet moments of your dining room: a brilliant magenta *Iresine herbstii* in a pale blue ceramic pot, with your pet collection of African violets in chorus at the base. In a winter sunny window the colors will become iridescent and you will have a completely fresh focal point. The *Iresine* has one- to two-inch translucent leaves, long and oval. They're notched at the top and have lighter-colored midribs and veins. *Iresine lindenii* has foliage with more true red hue. These jewel colors belie the unattractive Bloodleaf name, but its other common name, Chicken Gizzard, is even more outlandish; such a pretty plant deserves better in the naming department!

Iresine is not a demanding plant, either. Its requirements are about the same as geraniums and *Coleus*. Pot it in packaged soil and water only when the top soil feels dry to touch. Add misting to increase humidity. Pinch off the growing tips to keep its perky, bushy look.

Propagation: cuttings in fall.

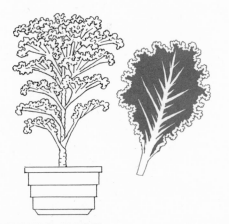

FLOWERING KALE

Cabbage plant in the dining room? Ahhh—but such a cabbage! This clumpy, homely garden vegetable has turned Cinderella, and comes to the table in gorgeous crinkly purple-green or creamy-white-with-lavender dress, as a dressy potted plant. Not only that, you may be asked to pay $5 for that pot, instead of the dime-a-pound, cook-pot type.

It grows a ballet skirt, layer on lacy layer of leaves, on a short stem. Set it in a big pewter or chrome ice bucket and fill the space between pot and bucket with sphagnum moss; or, repot in a Chinese basket which has been lined with plastic and layered on the bottom with charcoal. Several baskets on a buffet party table will make the room come alive.

Never let it wilt, and keep it out of direct sunlight. Soil should be slightly moist at all times. If the room gets too cool, it may start "bolting" or flowering.

Propagation: by seeds, fairly fast, in summer for winter fun; this is a learning plant for five- and six-year-olds to start. Buy transplants, pot up to four-inch and then six-inch pots.

JEWEL ORCHID

Haemaria discolor is an easy orchid grown for the color of its leaves rather than the bloom; they're rich green on top with deep red underleaf and veins. It has a soft velvet look which glows under candlelight, or filtered sun and a warm window location. A bench placed near an east exposure to hold a large terrarium planted with Jewel orchids offers a rare jewelry shop in your own dining area.

The *Haemaria* dotes on humidity and warmth; the rhizomes should be planted shallow—both good reasons to try the glass bowl container. Potting soil should be fern fibers, sphagnum, bark and beech leaves, or a good orchid mix. Soft water, particularly rainwater, is its delight.

The blossom appears on a hairy stem with a dozen or more small white flowers. The plant has to have a rest period or it won't bloom. Feed weekly during growing months. Mist daily, if the Jewel Orchid is grown in a shallow pot.

91

PLANTS FOR DULL DINING ROOMS

LEOPARD PLANT

Tame a leopard in your corner cupboard; domesticate your wild pet on a reed hassock in a cool north window. *Ligularia tussilaginea,* the Leopard plant, brought its broad showy leaves from the woods of Japan—and huzzah for the move!

The Leopard's leaves are a non-typical shape, the size of tea saucers, with shallow angles all around the edge and called by some Colt's Foot. They are enriched with golden flecks and patterns. Flower stalks, one to two feet tall, will appear and have a few yellow heads, one and a half to two inches across.

Pot this cool herbaceous beauty in a large white matte-glazed crock, with packaged soil. Keep it very moist in summer and almost dry from November to February. Although it likes cool, try to keep the thermostat above 60°, and don't worry about dry air.

Propagation: divide clump in February.

PURPLE HEART

The Wandering Jew family gets another medal for its Purple Heart, *Setcreasea purpurea* has a larger, simpler structure than *Zebrina, Tradescantia* or *Tripogandra,* and probably the handsomest coloration. It grows with indifferent attention, its long purple leaves lolling in the sun.

Purple Hearts grow on stems sharply vertical in the pot, but the weight of growth gives them a soft nudge over the side, making them admirable plants for a group of hanging baskets in a sunny window. Six or eight can distract the eye from a drab view or nosy neighbors, and you can start them all from cuttings which literally spring out of the soil. Pinching back the long hanging stems increases the center growth and encourages small, pale orchid flowers.

Keep Purple Hearts moderately dry between waterings; if they dry out, the leaves turn yellowish, but a good dunking will renew their vitality. Temperature range between 60° and 75° is fine, and four hours of sun will hold the deep color.

Propagation: stem cuttings.

TI PLANT

You can start a Ti from a two-inch pot bought for 49 cents or a larger 10-dollar pot from your garden center. The only difference is that you don't have to wait three or four years for the little one to grow up—and a big specimen will do more for the dining room right now. You can double pot it in a brass bowl from India, in your inherited silver punch bowl (filling the spaces around with cool moist moss), or sit it on top of a ceramic umbrella jar.

Ti, or *Cordyline terminalis,* comes from the South Pacific. A two-inch section will sprout quickly in moist sand kept at 80° on the bottom of the pot. New little plantlets respond faster.

The marvelously painted leaves are red, maroon, pink, dark green, and up to 18 inches long; they spiral up the trunk so you can see the tops and undersides from any point. Give Ti lots of sun, warm temperatures never below 60°, and high humidity. It can take low light but sun keeps the color fast. If it grows too rapidly cut off the top, and new growth will start right below the cut. *Cordyline stricta* is adaptable too, but has less color, takes less light.

VELVET PLANT

Another jewel for an elegant table centerpiece: *Gynura sarmentosa,* also called the Purple Passion vine. Find a spot where *Gynura* can get a half day's sun, and move to its centerpiece position at dinner.

93

Intense green iridescent leaves are covered with purple hairs which catch the sun—no plant has more mystery in its color. New leaves are brightest purple, turning more towards green with age; veins and edges are hairy, too. Stems are deep red and like to twine. The Velvet plant may get to be two feet tall and have small orange flowers. *Gynura aurantiaca,* Royal Velvet plant, is a shrub rather than a vine, has smaller leaves and can be pinched back to Tom Thumb size; it too has orange bloom. Both *Gynura* are adaptable as hanging basket show-offs.

Both are warmth lovers, 65° to 70° nights, and 75° to 85° days—great summer plants. Do your parental duty and keep them always barely moist, feeding sparingly once a month. Pinch back to keep from getting straggly. Those tips root easily. Repot in package potting soil in spring.

PLANTS FOR DULL DINING ROOMS

BEGONIA

Q *What's the right temperature for begonias indoors?*

A Moderation is the word: 60° to 65° at night and 65° to 72° during the day.

Q *What would make the edges of my begonia leaves get stiff and dry?*

A Begonias do not make it with a dry atmosphere. Bring them humidity and good ventilation. Stand your pots on trays lined with pebbles, add water, but don't let it touch the bottom of the pot. Don't mist because too much humidity can encourage fungus, particularly if the light level is not good. Avoid watering with hard water and beware of overwatering an Angel-Wing. Let the plant dry before watering again.

CALADIUM

Q *Why does my Caladium look sickly?*

A Your leaves could be looking "sickly" because they're coming to the end of their cycle. *Caladium* are active six to seven months out of the year, and then their leaves start to wither. Hold back on water then; remove the plant to an inconspicuous spot so you won't be unhappy about it. When you finally remove the plant from the pot, shake off soil, dust the tubers with a fungicide and store in dry peat in a cool place for four to five months. Divide before replanting. *Caladium* desire greenhouse conditions: warm moist 75° to 85° days, 65° to 70° nights, and thorough immersion watering by putting the pot in a pail until the bubbles stop. Give them bright light.

GERANIUM

Q *I feed my geraniums but there's no bloom.*

A Unless you give a fertilizer high in phosphorus, you'll get lots of green but little color. If the leaves look yellowish, they may need more feeding. Actually, geraniums take less feeding than most house plants, perhaps only once a month.

Q *Can I store geraniums in my basement when they look tired?*

A Only if your basement has a sunny window. They don't like the dark. Once they recover, you can make cuttings.

GLOXINIA

Q *I'm going to plant some Gloxinia tubers a neighbor gave me; how deep do I put them in the pot?*

A Use packaged soil, and pot the tuber so that the top shows above the soil. February is a good starting month, as long as the tuber has had a rest of at least two to three months.

Q *Some of the buds on my Gloxinia get brown and do nothing.*

A Overwatering, watering with cold water, or thrips can be the problem. The moisture factor is important: *Gloxinia* likes humidity, warmth, and wet-to-dry watering. Don't let the ground get soggy; it can cause tubers to rot.

MINIATURE ROSE

Q *I lost the instructions for growing my miniature roses. Can you tell me what I should do to keep them blooming?*

A You can grow these charming little bloomers under fluorescent lights, keeping the lights about six inches from the foliage. The natural way is to grow them in a south window with sun. They like moisture and ventilation. Mist them daily. They seem to benefit from an insecticide/fungicide spraying monthly. Fertilize once a month, too.

Q *Do I put my little roses outdoors in the summer?*

A They like the air movement so it's a good idea in moderate climates; bring them inside in the fall. Watch for snails outside—they love the tender young leaves.

ORCHID

Q *What is the reason for the dark spots which appear all of a sudden on the leaves?*

A It may be sunburn. Orchids do best in bright light in summer, and in a sunny location in winter. If the spots are not rigid like the leaf, but limp, it could be fungus; treat with a fungicide after you cut out the black part.

Q *The leaves on my orchid are slightly yellow. Should I feed them something?*

A This may come from over-fertilizing. I suggest you water the pots well to leach out the excess fertilizer and hold off further feeding for a month. Orchids do better with less than more.

Q *Buds form on my Cymbidium and then fall off.*

A This plant needs a temperature change down to 50° to 60° at night to assure completion of blossoming. Misting helps, but do it early in the day so that leaves are not wet at night.

Q *My son gave me an orchid for Mother's Day last year and the roots are coming out of the top of the pot. Does this mean it should be repotted?*

A This is normal for most Orchids. Repotting will keep the blooming away for a year, so enjoy and don't worry.

SPATHIPHYLLUM

Q *My Spathiphyllum has stopped blooming. It was so pretty—how can I get it to bloom again?*

A Normal flowering time is January through March, but some will go right through summer. Divide and pot in late fall, in two parts peat, one sharp sand and one of packaged soilless mixture. Keep it warmish and in bright light, and you should get repeat action. Keep moist, too, except when the plant is resting.

TI PLANT

Q *Does my Ti plant have to be in the sun?*

A No, it will grow in bright light or moderate, but sun makes the colors sing.

VELVET PLANT

Q *Is it true I can mist the Velvet plant? I thought plants with hairy leaves shouldn't get wet.*

A Yes, *Gynura* seems to like the addition of man-made humidity, but it is an exception to the rule. It does well with evenly moist soil, too.

STRIPED
TREEBINE

GOLDEN
TRUMPET

BABY'S CRIB WITH
LEGS REMOVED

CLOCK VINE

ASPIDISTRA

96

POTS OF
CAMPANULA

**PLANTS FOR BEDROOMS
WITH HANG-UPS**

Where do *you* sleep? In a twin-bed room? On a Murphy fold-up in a one-room convenience? In a sleeping bag or hammock strung out in a VW bus? A canopied four-poster in a 200-year old alcove? In a middle-of-the-living-room waterbed? A single cot in a retirement home?

I don't know about you, but the room where I sleep has space only for a bed and a long Chinese coffee table under a west window for plants and books—and a flood of late afternoon sun to melt away tensions. It's an end-of-the-day place to escape telephones, to catch up on stacks of unread magazines. The west bay window has had a brilliant red-blooming *Kalanchoe,* two feet tall, performing for five months; a Mistletoe fig in a stone bowl and a blooming *Oxalis* sit on the table. In the north bay window which looks out on typical San Francisco back stairs there's a Ming fern which loves the cool north light, a *Cotoneaster* from Australia and a seedling *Beaucarnea.*

None of these plants are related, the forms are mismatched; but each is a personality I like, and they seem to like me. Their containers are old things I love—a Chinese plum jar wrapped in crisscross bamboo strips, a square ebony box lined with copper, a stone bowl turned and glazed by a friend. The containers make them agreeable relatives. These things spell *peace.* And if there's one room where you seek that, it's the room where you sleep—particularly if you are a parent.

One plant can change a bedroom. A dozen, hanging from the ceiling in a checkerboard pattern (provided you own the house) can make a bower. Two Clock vines, sitting on short lengths of an old telephone pole (painted dark blue or brown), are lifted up so you see them first thing in the a.m., and when you drift off at night. A baby's crib repainted and filled with eight or ten heliotrope or primroses in bloom is a miniature nursery. Suspend a white string macrame hanger holding a single *Lotus berthelotii* in a wicker basket, and that room is no longer just a room.

Think about it. Is the room *you* sleep in only a room? If there's no place other than a windowsill for pots, make the sill a wide shelf with the addition of a board and brackets under to hold it. If there's a

PLANTS FOR BEDROOMS

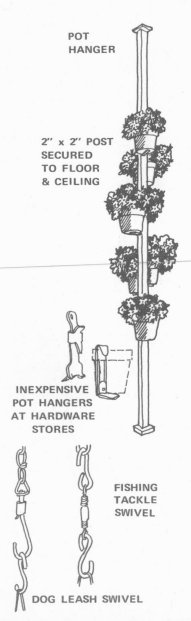

POT
HANGER

2" x 2" POST
SECURED
TO FLOOR
& CEILING

INEXPENSIVE
POT HANGERS
AT HARDWARE
STORES

FISHING
TACKLE
SWIVEL

DOG LEASH SWIVEL

radiator underneath the window to contend with, put insulation between that and the shelf. Hang plants in front of windows at different levels; hang them in front of mirrors. If you're a handyman and you own the window, look for the pre-fab greenhouse, window-size, which you can install yourself, and fill the opening with scores of plants.

Take the door off a closet and consolidate your wardrobe—or call in the Salvation Army. Put fluorescent lighting in the alcove and hang a mass of *Cissus* vines. Build plant stands out of sturdy cartons covered with contact paper and try low-light ferns at the cooler floor level. Imagine waking up in your own plant shop.

Find an unused bookcase, refinish it to harmonize with the wall-paper behind: A whole collection of African violets or *Streptocarpus* will fill shelves with bloom if you install a tube light under each shelf to light the one below. If your sense of humor needs a lift, shop for an old wooden potty-chair, sand it to a bare-wood look and put a large Piggyback in that obvious hole.

Don't fill a bedside table so that you knock off a pot every time you fight the alarm. Plants should be seen and not hurt. *Don't* decorate with plants; put them near you because you feel something nice is happening. Cater to yourself, your plant children. About the plants to grow where you sleep: they should be soft, pleasant, friendly. No pointy *Yucca* or *Aloe,* no coarse *Dracaena* or Rubber tree here. Go shopping for one big green, if you have the space, like a cool-room Umbrella plant, *Cyperus alternifolius gracilis* (see Plants for Skinny Spaces) or a Butterfly palm (see the section on Palms). Sleeping on the floor will be good for your back, at least until you can afford the palm *and* the mattress. Shop for happy vine types which bloom, like *Ampelopsis;* the tender tendrils lull and soothe.

In addition to the plants described on the following pages, other plants for bedrooms with hang-ups are: *Impatiens, Episcia, Fuchsia,* ivy, Rosary vine, Strawberry geranium, *Lantana,* Wandering Jew, *Clerodendrum,* Flowering Maple, Passion vine(!).

BASKET AMPELOPSIS

If you wake up late some morning and discover the *Ampelopsis* dangling its twiny tendrils down by your ear—just ignore, and get ready to prune. This endearing and rapid-growing climber is an offside relative of the Virginia Creeper and will need a strong hand to keep it inside the room. In ideal situations, it will even produce brilliant blue berries, hence the nickname Blueberry Climber.

Ampelopsis brevipedunculata is a deciduous vine outside, but with T.L.C. should hold on to leaves in a cool sleep room. Once the temperature rises, particularly in fall, the leaves turn red, and may split, as the current phrase goes. Its delicate miniature grape leaves of dark green cover pink, slightly hairy stems.

As a hanging plant, it softens any corner. But put it on a trellis or a lattice screen painted white, in front of a window, and you have the perfect answer for the no-curtain look. The screen lets in the cheery sun-and-shadow pattern of a rarely simple foliage to contemplate of an early morning. *Ampelopsis vitace* has marbled leaves.

Cut back to the woody trunk if it defoliates, otherwise depend on pinching back to keep it acceptable. Takes sun or shade.

Propagation: seeds, or green wood cuttings.

CLOCK VINE

Also called Black-Eyed Susan vine, *Thunbergia alata* is a showy, brassy wench with knockout orange petals shaped in a flat collar with deep violet or black centers—real morning brighteners. It has stiff spear-shaped leaves on vining three-inch stems. Try *Thunbergia* in hanging pots, or as a round-the-year bloomer on a pedestal or on a glass shelf in a south window. It will need vertical support.

Clock vine is a perennial which lives the easy life if the warmth is in the 50° to 72° range. Never let it dry out; give heavy watering hand and misting. Full sunlight makes it tick. It grows with exuberance—cut back too-long trailers to encourage more bloom. Its only annoyance: red spider mites which should respond to a soapy solution spray.

Propagation: try seeding in sand and peat moss in late winter, keeping the seeds evenly damp, in good light. Transplant into a good potting mix when the plants are about four inches tall.

99

PLANTS FOR BEDROOMS

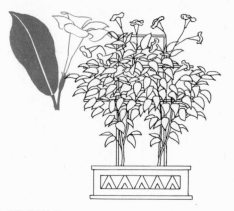

DIPLADENIA

Another delicate climber to provide privacy in an east or west window of a bed chamber. Romantically twining, *Dipladenia splendens* will reach six feet or more indoors, dripping with big pink-to-crimson flowers, perhaps four inches wide. There is controversy over the label: Some call it *Mandevilla "Alice du Pont,"* and what you find on the tag depends on the nurseryman's source. *Dipladenia boliviensis* has lovely white trumpet flowers with yellow throats.

Dipladenia would be a prize hanging swinger in an old bird cage stand beside the dressing table. It goes with pretty flowered sheets, white wicker chairs and needlepoint rugs. Pot several in a reed fernery and fill spaces around the pots with sphagnum moss. Add vertical supports of nylon fish line, secured to the window frame.

Characteristically a greenhouse vine, *Dipladenia* is sensitive to cold, responding to rich soil with good drainage, weekly feeding spring and summer (always to damp soil) and east or west sun. Mist on hot days; if leaves curl, either the light is too bright or the air is too dry. Cut back in February to encourage young-blooming shoots.

Propagation: cuttings.

GOLDEN TRUMPET

Allamanda grandiflora is a Brazilian import. Although a jungle twiner, it will do beautifully next to a window facing south. I can see it on a low footstool, with grandpa's cane set in between the *Allamanda* pot and a larger pot or basket to support the heavy vine. Add a low rocker, a knitting basket and good light, and the picture develops.

The Golden Trumpet is evergreen, and its intense dark foliage needs pinching back occasionally. *A. grandiflora* has golden yellow tubes or funnels which flare to three inches, and white throats. It blooms continuously from April through summer, sharing its delicate fragrance.

Golden Trumpet loves light from a south window and generous watering, including a misting every couple of days. Feed weekly in summer. Cut back in February, and start new plants from the cuttings. Application of bottom heat to the cuttings will speed up their growth.

ITALIAN BELLFLOWER

A fragile-stemmed perennial, *Campanula isophylla* has lovely large star-shape flowers—just the sort of tender expression you might expect from the Italians. Its curly short stems have down-covered muted green leaves, and though seemingly tender, *Campanula* speaks in impassioned purple. *Campanula alba* has pristine white trumpets.

A hanging cachepot with purple and white intertwining in front of a sunny window revives the tired mind. If the sleeping room is ample, an old cradle filled with *Campanula* to overflow is breathtaking.

Because the cuttings propagate simply, start a dozen new plants in spring. Strong alkaline soil is called for, with some gravel for increased drainage. Fertilize lightly every week, April through July. Heavy watering in summer; keep almost dry and very cool after bloom and during the late winter (or the next blossoms will be scarce). Also, watch for fungus from too-damp air or soil. Repot in February.

PARROT'S BEAK

The name belies its delicacy. *Lotus berthelotii* is an herbaceous mist of silver down and finely divided leaves. When it cascades from white macrame slings, perhaps four or five plants at different heights, the whole room becomes an oasis, a joy to use for midday secret naps and snatch-reading.

Parrot's Beak comes from the Canary Islands, and is also known as Winged Pea. The rich scarlet beaks appear along the stems in April and May, like so many butterflies in the clouds. It loves the sun and will illuminate your bower far into fall. Then there may be a fallout at the top, and for a few months it is better off resting in some cool location. Substitute another viner like Striped Treebine for winter, and come spring, with weekly feedings, the *Lotus* can emerge once more.

Regular watering to keep the soil slightly moist is imperative. When allowed to dry out, leaves will shed. Repotting in late summer is a good idea; packaged soil will do. The wintering should take place with temperatures around 45° to 55°.

Propagation: by seed, or young shoots in spring.

PLANTS FOR BEDROOMS

STRIPED TREEBINE

Cissus relatives are all candidates for sleep areas, the dressing room or the guest powder room. They are vigorous climbers, trailers, which live contentedly in semi-shade or by a window with no direct sun. Striped Treebine, *Cissus striata,* is a more uncommon one which emigrated from Japan. Its untamed branching has dainty five-finger leaves spaced so that each is distinct, patterny. Backlight it and the changing forms never cease to fascinate.

Cissus antarctica, Kangaroo vine, is a bedroom natural and likes shade. *Cissus discolor* from Java has heart-shaped light olive leaves with silver markings on the edges and red underneath; new leaves are violet-purple. *Rhoicissus rhomboidea,* Natal vine, is a glistening and vigorous performer which takes poor light but lots of space.

The *Cissus* family members don't mind an indifferent waterer, except in winter when they should be underwatered. They all plant up well in garden soil mixed with sand, no peat. Feed weekly. One warning: Keep away from heaters, radiators—they hate heat (60° is happiness).

Propagation: young shoots in April. Pruning these encourages fullness in the plant.

WAX PLANT

There are two popular types of the Wax plant or vine, *Hoya bella* and *Hoya carnosa,* both with rich polished leaves and flowers that look like nosegays.

Hoya bella is the daintier of the two, with smaller pointed leaves, and long-lasting pale pink blossoms which hang down. These exquisite blooms masquerade as wax facsimiles when they first appear. Then, one day, they burst open, blushing velvet stars with purple throats, in a rounded cluster which will stay on for four or five months. A word of warning: If you cut off a cluster, no bloom will reappear at that point again. New bloom comes only to the old knotty perennial stems.

Hang it high; hang three in a group near your bed to enjoy the elusive fragrance and to look up into them.

The Wax plant requires good light but shade from sun, and does fine in warm temperatures (it comes from Java). Moderate watering is the formula, except that from October to January it should stay almost dry. Try misting on hot days. Feed monthly with a high phosphate-potash formula.

Repot young plants each spring, older ones only when crowding out of the pot. One susceptibility: mealy bugs. Keep an eye-watch for any signs of the little devils.

Propagation: cuttings, in spring.

AFRICAN VIOLET

Q *Is it all right to leave my African violet in a plastic pot?*

A Yes. Clay, ceramic and plastic all seem to do equally well. But most important, the pot needs to be sterilized before putting in the plant to kill any possible fungi action. Three- and four-inch pots are adequate for most violets. Squatty types are best to match these shallow-rooted plants.

Q *What would make my violet leaves turn yellow?*

A There are several possibilities: over fertilizing, overwatering, too dry atmosphere. Setting a violet on a moist pebble tray will up the humidity it requires. Avoid sun and cold drafts.

BROWALLIA

Q *Someone gave me Browallia seeds. When do I plant them?*

A During the summer; start them in moist peat and sand with a plastic tent over to hold in moisture. Bring indoors after you've potted up in September. Keep roots cool in the pot when the rest of the plant is in the sun. You can do this by double-potting, and filling the space between the two pots with moist sphagnum.

CAMPANULA

Q *Does the Campanula bloom all year indoors?*

A I've never heard of that all-out gymnastics. You'll probably get bushels of bloom from August into early winter. Then cut back the older stems and keep the plant cool for at least two months, with just enough water to survive. Repot in March, dividing to make two pots; fertilize, step up watering and start the sunny cycle once more.

FIRECRACKER VINE

Q *Will my Firecracker vine bloom again next year?*

A Yes, it should. However, young plants will put out more for you. When you pinch back the older *Manettia*, root the tips. Repeat pinching in young plants, and within six months they may explode.

FLAME VIOLET

Q *My Flame Violet has long runners but it doesn't have any blossoms.*

A The *Episcia* is so busy making those runners it has no energy left: cut back and wait for counteraction. If the plant is getting bald-headed in the center, wind some of the runners around inside the pot, pinning down to the soil so they will root and fill the voids.

FUCHSIA

Q *I have good luck with fuchsias in the garden but they won't do anything in the house. Why?*

A They need cool nights for at least three months before they set flowers; your house may be too warm. Also, *Fuchsia* need plenty of room to grow. It's a good idea to repot yearly in January or February and to prune out the deadwood. When spring comes, pinch back the tips of new growth to increase bushiness. Watch for blooms in two months.

PLANTS FOR BEDROOMS

HOLLY FERN

Q *What would be a good bedroom fern?*

A Holly fern, *Crytomium falcatum,* is a dark green fern with large holly-shape leaves on the gracefully arching fronds. It can take more warmth or cold and less humidity than the other ferns. It will be pleased if you give it a shower once a week to wash the leaves and supply moisture. Ferns like Maidenhair and Boston are too demanding of special conditions; try the Holly.

LANTANA

Q *I had Lantana in a pot on my back porch but it hasn't done anything since I brought it in. Why?*

A Older plants lose their virility. You can try cutting back, but I'd suggest starting new plants from cuttings or seeds in summer. Also, if you cut off *Lantana* buds before bringing indoors, there's a better chance for bloom later.

PASSION VINE

Q *Could I keep a Passion vine in the house all year?*

A You can keep almost any plant indoors if conditions are what the plant likes most, but most of us won't compromise our own comfort. *Passiflora* will develop buds in late winter inside after a fall rest period with reduced watering and cool quarters, and a month following that in a sunny spring window. Put it outdoors in summer in a warm location, if only a shelf outside the window. Give it vine supports; then bring it back inside when you want to drool over the luscious blooms. Cuttings rooted in water will bloom the first year.

PATIENT LUCY

Q *I grow Patient Lucy in the shade on my patio. Will it take shade in the house? Is that why my plant looks puny?*

A They need sunny exposure indoors, and lots of moisture. About the smallness of *Impatiens* plants: Perhaps you have a variety which is a mini. Check the seed packet or the nursery label for information about eventual growth.

ROSARY VINE

Q *Can I get more Rosary vines if I cut off those little knobs on the stems and plant them?*

A Those little "knobs" on the *Ceropegia* are tubers, and can be potted up. You can also divide the tuberous roots, as well as find success growing from stem cuttings.

STRAWBERRY GERANIUM

Q *Every Strawberry geranium I buy gets little spiders.*

A That would be the red spider mite, a nasty pest. Try a cooler temperature, more humidity, and mist a couple of times each day. *Saxifraga* is a cool-house baby. Also, wash the sill or area where the other plants stood with a household bleach solution to make it all antiseptic for the new geranium.

Q *How can I make a Strawberry geranium fuller near the roots?*

A Take a couple of runners and wind them around inside the pot; then pin them down with a hairpin or a paper clip cut in half. If there are any little plantlets on the runners, pin them down, too.

PLANTS TO FERN-ISH A BATH

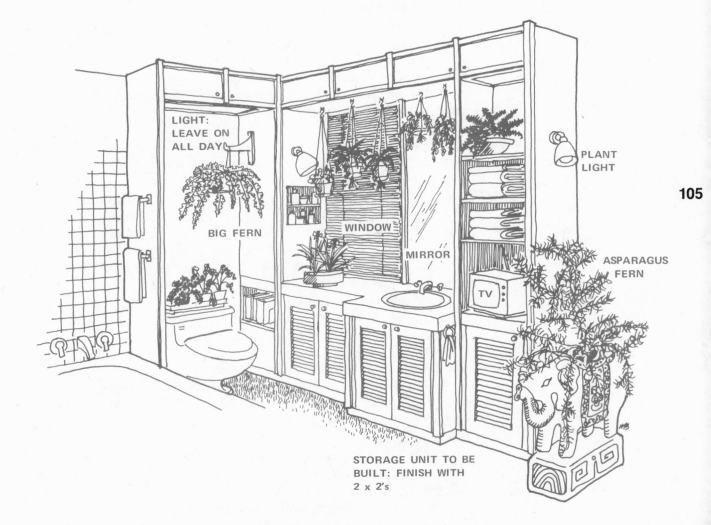

LIGHT: LEAVE ON ALL DAY

BIG FERN

WINDOW

MIRROR

PLANT LIGHT

ASPARAGUS FERN

TV

STORAGE UNIT TO BE BUILT: FINISH WITH 2 x 2's

FERNS FOR BATHROOMS

Have you walked into a friend's bathroom lately where the green is turned on? Wandering Jew pots hang from the shower rod, instead of pantyhose. Grape ivy flutters in front of a window, instead of plastic cottage curtains. A row of Bird's Nest ferns lines the top of the toilet tank to replace the liniment bottle and box of curlers.

Did it do anything for you? Did you recognize that any thought exercises you were having outside that door vanished inside the leafy grotto? There is a refreshing cleansing of the mind which green growing things dispense, particularly when they are catalysts to a bare tub, toilet and basin.

Early in the 20th century the toilet moved indoors to join the bathtub; the bathroom became a room with a door and a window, and very little else. It wasn't until some manufacturer started dyeing terry towels in colors and printing on them pretty (but scratchy) designs, and someone else colored the tissue boxes, that the antiseptic look began to fade. Someone else added magazine racks and printed shower curtains. Color tiles and colored basins still couldn't take the chill off that room. One day recently, someone must have said: Let there be plants. And now, the bathroom will never again be just a room.

Here is a perfectly good substitute for a greenhouse where plants flourish. Here is warmth, moisture, and if there is a sunny window, the very best place in the house or apartment to grow house plants. Ferns and water-growing plants, shy little-leaf plants like Tahitian Bridal Veil and Creeping fig, bold statements like the Umbrella plant which keeps its feet wet in a corner of the shower will lift an ordinary personal service area into a conservatory. Every time you walk through a door where the green is turned on, you'll wonder how you ever lived with a segregated bath.

Before you rush out and spend all your tax refund monies on Ming ferns and Mother Spleenworts, there are critical things to check: Where will you put plants which will not get in your way in the early morning rush hour? How will you deal with a plant which hangs on the shower rod—when you take a shower? If you hang a Parrot's Beak, will it get in your hair every time you stand up straight? Is there a spot where you can stand a tall bamboo or Parlor palm in a skinny corner? Would two or three glass shelves in front of the window to hold a collection of small ferns suit the limited space better than two or three ivies hanging at different heights?

The clue is once again to *really* look at the room. Then look at your budget. One important plant can hatch a host of follow-up ideas. If there's room for such a special, spend as much time as necessary to get one which will thrive in a warm damp room, and also accept the other parts of the day when the thermometer drops.

Lighting is the next consideration after temperature and humidity. Leaving a light on all day will supply what most greens require because of the extended time it is lit plus whatever the window provides. A fern which can hang over a tub will thank you for moving it close to that window when you're not using the room. The combined light will insure ruffled fern leaves on a Roosevelt fern which might hesitate to develop with less light. The all-day-light energy consumption is practically nil compared to the pleasure of the turned-on greens.

In addition to the plants described on the following pages, other plants for fern-ishing a bath are: ferns like *Davallia,* Holly, *Polystichum,* Boston, Staghorn, *Selaginella;* Norfolk pine, *Aspidistra,* palms, Rex begonias, African violets, bromeliads. Stay away from geraniums and plants which are happier dry.

FERNS FOR BATHROOMS

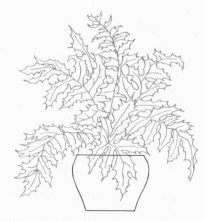

FLUFFY RUFFLES FERN

An old-fashioned lacy relative of the Boston, Fluffy Ruffles grows stiffly upright instead of arching. It is less the swinger and more properly sits on a white wicker plant pedestal to complement a stark white shower stall, or blue and white Dutch tiles.

Put *Nephrolepis exaltata "Fluffy Ruffles"* near a sunny window but out of the direct rays. Mist it several times daily during warm spells and it will come through full and fresh. That same faithful misting is essential in winter when the furnace is on and humidity drops. Overwatering does not solve humidity, but setting a fern pot on a moist pebble tray helps, and so does misting. Water deeply by dunking the pot in the tub or basin for at least 10 minutes, then drain well; fern roots can drown from lack of oxygen in soggy soil.

Be a good plant parent and trim the old outside fronds when they turn brown; cut back to the base of the stem. The average life of a frond is about nine months. New growth comes from the middle of the plant. Keep Fluffy Ruffles fat and growing with a monthly application of high-nitrogen solution after winter dormancy is ended, and until September.

Propagation: cut off runners which self-root, and pot up.

HARE'S FOOT FERN

Polypodium aureum mandaianum is also labeled False Hare's Foot by some botanists. False or real, it is a knockout and one of those big exuberant crested ferns whose bluish color sets it apart from the mob. Grow it in a hanging basket with an open pattern and those telltale "hare's feet" hairy rhizomes will push out and around in fantastic patterns. A really fine specimen, given ideal conditions, will span three to five feet. Nothing false there! Because of its rangy size, most bathrooms can only accept it as a hanger; a low location could create a space crisis.

The Hare's Foot is easy to grow compared to ferns like the Boston, and has a much more intriguing form, I think. The sturdy, unmarked leaflets have wavy-toothed edges. *Polypodium* takes dappled or filtered light, can tolerate 50° nights and 72° when the shower is occupied. Like the other ferns, treat it to an always-moist-but-never-wet porous soil. Drainage is extra critical; packaged soil should include a lot of peat moss. To get more frond action, cut back some of the more active rhizomes to redistribute energy.

Propagation: division of rhizomes or by means of spores (complicated and slow).

MING FERN

This fern-which-is-not-a-fern also does not grow and flow like the rest of its *Asparagus* relatives. Ming fern is shrubby, with a gnarled trunk and slim zigzag branches with short puffs of bright green needles. *Asparagus retrofractus* is a self-determining character with bonsai tendencies. Needles appear after a sudden spurt of a new stem, and although some of the older ones fall, this fern is always delightfully full and far out. If the Ming attains a maturity, it will promise clusters of white bloom.

Packaged potting mix with peat moss or ground bark added is the recommended soil. Give evenly moist watering (if your water is hard or has been chemically softened, save rainwater, or give the Ming the bottled kind). Supply a cool spot, occasional misting and bright light, and a Ming fern will jolly up a bath, powder room, bedroom, entrance or even the harpsichord. Feed in March, June and September; if you have just adopted it, wait three to four months before feeding.

Propagation: division of fleshy roots of old plants. Cut back the stems to soil level because new ones will replace them.

ROUNDLEAF FERN

If you are the least bit nervous about sharing your shampoo time with a fern-watcher, let me recommend the modest little *Pellaea rotundifolia.* It is one of the "cliff-brakes," or coarser ferns.

The flat rosette grows to full size in a three-inch pot. Fronds rarely grow longer than 12 inches, usually shorter. They are intense green and simpler than most ferns; each stem has two rows of button-shape frondlets. The last ones on the line are very delicate and when you water, do it gently so they don't break off. Because of its rosette, place it low, for the best overlook, perhaps on the clothes hamper, or on an upside-down wastebasket. If you know someone in the display department of an apparel store, ask for a discarded hosiery "leg" and install the *Pellaea* pot in the top of it.

Filtered shade or the bright light of a north window will suit a Roundleaf. Keep the soil barely moist, keep the fronds misted and don't worry if the bathroom cools off because this fern can take real blue-finger temperatures. Fertilize sparingly with fish emulsion, using less than half the amount recommended on the label.

Propagation: spores.

109

FERNS FOR BATHROOMS

SILVER FERN

This is one of the "brake," or coarse ferns, commonly called table ferns. *Pteris quadriaurita 'Argyraea'* is certainly not limited to a table: it may be
grown on glass shelves in front of a bathroom window, hanging by the medicine cabinet, or in a reed fernery to make a happy freshener for early morning grumpies. If your powder room is cut off from bright light, hang several Silvers close to the light fixture and leave it on all day while you're away.

Silver fern is a native of India, and has tall fronds which are rather coarsely divided. The fronds are offbeat with their strange white markings, and plant up interestingly with the little flat Roundleaf with its dark form.

This particular brake fern seems to relish winter sunlight and curtain-filtered summer daylight. Like ferns in general, misting is called for to keep up the humidity level. Keep barely moist; put Silvers under the shower once a week to keep them bright and happy, and to discourage insect problems. Feed twice a year, about half the amount recommended by the manufacturer. Ferns can't handle overeating. Never fertilize a newly bought plant; wait six months.

Propagation: spores, or by division.

VICTORIA FERN

Victoria is another "brake" fern, a sword-brake, but despite that tough name it is the beauty of the family. *Pteris ensiformis victoriae* is slim, compact, fresh-looking. As a dwarf form, Victoria will sit regally on the ceramic top of your W.C., in a Wedgwood or Royal Doulton cachepot. Its frondlets are delicately rounded with a silvery strip following the middle vein and outlined with dark green edges.

Victoria ferns rarely need a pot larger than five inches. Make sure they have good drainage. When you double pot, that is put the fern pot inside another larger container, add a layer of pebbles in the bottom of the latter so that the fern's feet never stand in overflow water. Check the pebble condition occasionally to be sure there's no stagnant water to smell or breed mosquitoes.

If a fern is doing well, don't worry it with moving. (A short trip to the wash basin to submerge the pot once a week for a thorough dunking doesn't count.) Like any fern, the Victoria likes good light; limited light will slow growth but be tolerated. Culture for the Victoria is generally the same as for the Silver.

Propagation: spores, or by division.

BIRD'S NEST FERN

Q *I've had a Bird's Nest fern for a year and it doesn't seem to grow like the ones at my florist's.*

A The florist and the nursery have cool moist greenhouse conditions which the *Asplenium nidus* loves. It's hard to duplicate that in your own home. Misting is a must with ferns in dry-heat apartments and houses, and the added humidity lowers the temperature. Look for the coolest bright spot and award it to your fern. Also, feed it at least every three weeks with a half portion of liquid fish emulsion.

BOSTON FERN

Q *Boston ferns are so expensive now. Can I divide the one I have to make two plants?*

A Boston types, the *Nephrolepis* group, are hard to divide successfully and only an old fern hand should try. What you can do takes longer, but costs you only the price of a pot: Find the runners or shoots which grow across the top of the Boston's pot and pin them down with a U-shape pin or half a paper clip. These runners root quickly, and in a couple of months form new plants which can be cut off and potted.

Q *The outer leaves of my Boston are raggedy. Can I cut them off?*

A To answer your question: Yes, you can cut them off, close to the top of the roots. The fronds have a life span of about nine months, and the ones on the outside are the oldest because the fern grows from the center. The next layer of leaves will move into their place and by taking off the old, new fronds will grow fuller and faster.

HARE'S FOOT FERN

Q *Is there any way to encourage a Hare's Foot to fill in some of the open spaces in the pot?*

A If you cut back some of the hairy rhizomes of the *Polypodium* that are creeping at the base of the plant, the energy will transfer to frond making.

HOLLY FERN

Q *Is there any trick to repotting a Holly fern?*

A When the *Cyrtomium* shows signs of overcrowding, repot in early spring in equal parts of packaged soil, peat moss and leaf mold. Be very careful not to set the fern lower in the pot than the depth it grew before, and firm the soil gently around the roots, mounding up to the beginnings of the stems. Don't feed for at least six months.

MAIDENHAIR FERN

Q *I don't seem to have luck growing Maidenhair.*

A Your problem is commoner than you know. This is a very touchy fern to tackle because it has to have consistently moist, cool location, and few families can live in a greenhouse all the time. If you have a rarely used guest room or a lean-to greenhouse, you can meet its demands. *Adiantum* likes bright light, no sun and a sandy-humusy mixture. So, don't try it unless you're a sweater-wearing cool bird.

FERNS FOR BATHROOMS

MING FERN

Q *My new Ming fern's needles are turning yellow.*

A The *Asparagus retrofractus* may need more light; try an uncurtained north window. Also, if it has dried out, needles will turn color and drop. Always keep it evenly moist.

MOTHER FERN

Q *I have a Mother fern in my terrarium and would like to know how to propagate those little bulblets which grow on the leaves.*

A You can pick them off and pot the bulbs any time of the year. Put a quarter-inch layer of charcoal in the bottom of a pot, add a mixture of half packaged soil, half peat moss, and plant the bulblet. Cover with a polyethylene film to make a mini-terrarium until the plant takes hold. Then provide it with the high humidity and warmth which *Asplenium bulbiferum* enjoys. Do not fertilize for at least six months.

OUTDOORS

Q *Can I put ferns outdoors in summer?*

A Yes, in a shady spot, out of wind and sun. And don't forget to water them.

PALE LEAVES

Q *Why do leaves on a table fern get paler?*

A If the fern has been overexposed to the sun or the air has been too dry, it will affect the color of the fronds. So will underwatering. I have been told (but haven't tried it) that cold tea instead of plain water, applied once a week, gives a fern just the right amount of acid to keep it greening.

SPORES

Q *How complicated is it to grow ferns from spores?*

A It all depends on what you mean by complicated. It takes patience, discipline and time. First of all, the container and soil mixture the spores will grow in must be in an antiseptic condition. This is to remove bacteria and fungus spores. Boil a large kettle of water, let it cool and saturate the pot in it. Use some of it to moisten the soil. If you use garden soil, it should be baked in the oven (see section on Soil) and sifted through a piece of window screening. In a large container put two parts of this soil, two parts of peat moss which has been sifted, and one part sharp sand, and mix well.

Watch for the fern spore cases to start opening. Put the cut fronds in a brown paper bag until the powdery spores drop. Dust the spores over the soil-filled pot, carefully pressing down, and cover the moistened soil with polyethylene film. Protect from sun, and keep at about 70°. A heart-shaped green "prothallium" appears first; from that the real fern develops. Keep the pot moist and covered while this happens, which will be about six months, then remove it; pot up the new ferns when they have grown good healthy roots and are at least an inch and a half.

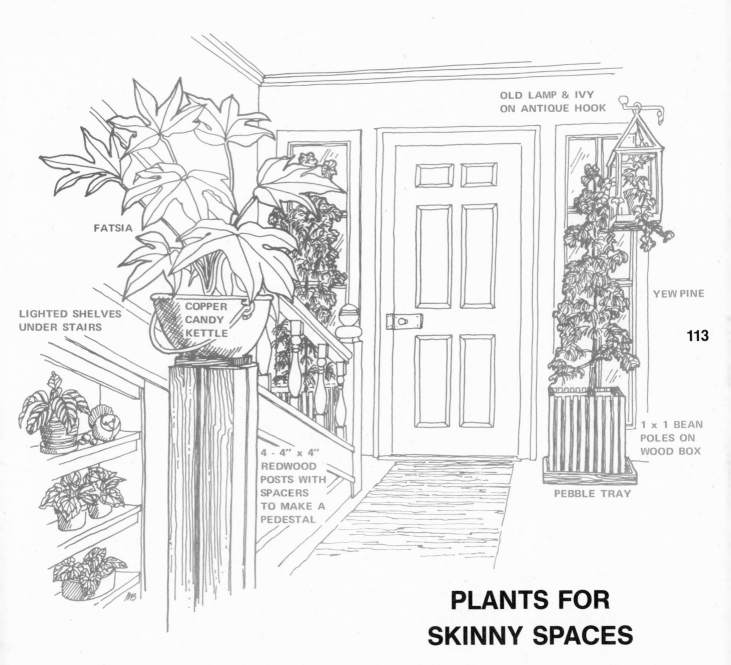

OLD LAMP & IVY
ON ANTIQUE HOOK

FATSIA

LIGHTED SHELVES
UNDER STAIRS

COPPER
CANDY
KETTLE

YEW PINE

113

4 - 4" x 4"
REDWOOD
POSTS WITH
SPACERS
TO MAKE A
PEDESTAL

1 x 1 BEAN
POLES ON
WOOD BOX

PEBBLE TRAY

**PLANTS FOR
SKINNY SPACES**

PLANTS FOR SKINNY SPACES

Funny thing about being a plant parent: Most people begin by adopting baby plants, moving cautiously to six- and eight-inch pots. It simply wouldn't occur to indulge affection on a great skinny basketball type! Most of us opt for a hanging plant because we have a place for a hanger. Or, we choose something small for a known windowsill. But something really tall—for space which never occurred to the imagination—boggles the budget.

That's why this break-down-inhibitions section is included. There are all kinds of spots you've probably never considered introducing to a tall plant: Take the stair landing of an old house, an apartment; there's usually a window (because designers reckoned the fall-ability of dark stairs). Take the entrance of many homes where there is a tall "light," or window, next to the door. Take an entrance hall with nothing but the rug on the floor. Take wall space behind the TV in the family room or bedroom. Take the spot in front of the non-moving door of a pair of glass doors to a patio or deck, or the narrow space between two doors in the kitchen. Take the barebones balcony, the fire escape. Is there a skylighted hallway, a dressing room corner? A swimming pool enclosure or a basement room with good light, warmth? Do you need a distraction plant to reroute traffic?

Think *tall* for limited spaces. Most of the plants recommended here are not all that expensive, nor are they hyper problems. The Chinese *Podocarpus*, the *Fatshedera*, the oleander, the Algerian ivy come from a nursery growing outdoor plants, for about the same price of a blooming azalea. It's a matter of acclimating them to indoor living.

If you're still not sold on the idea of this unusual adoption, buy or build a pedestal, four feet high and at least 10 inches in each of the other dimensions, and put a trailing plant on top to get the effect. A big Boston fern will give you a sample of what can happen.

But don't stop there. If you can, find a vertical-growing Parlor palm, or if you live in the South, pot up a clump of sugarcane or talk a friend into splitting with his Golden Cane bamboo. These plants make immediate magic for the narrow space. I have envied a woman in San

Francisco who has a blooming white *Bougainvillea* growing in a narrow window corner of a bedroom. Sophistication is the only word for a giant Pencil cactus six or seven feet tall standing by a floor-to-ceiling glass wall. The *Fatshedera* will look great just outside a balcony door. The Chinese *Podocarpus* and *Mahonia lomariifolia* will do well by you in an entrance foyer.

What if you already have 50 plants? Why do I push tall ones now? I would say of plant parents I've known, those with big "families" are always sneaking into greenery shops looking for something unlike anything they have. It is the same motivation which attacks stamp collectors and numismatists. Only now, *size* is the difference, and it opens a fascinating objective; leave behind your concepts about a planted pot and what's in it, in exchange for a new understanding of what one object gives to the space it shares.

In addition to the plants described on the following pages, other plants for skinny spaces are: *Osmanthus,* myrtle, Coffee tree, cacti, *Dizygotheca,* Rubber plant, Corn palm.

115

A 2-WHEEL CART IS THE EASIEST WAY TO HANDLE TALL PLANTS.

PLANTS FOR SKINNY SPACES

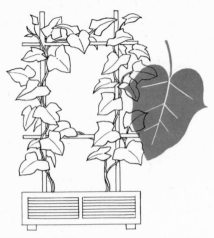

ALGERIAN IVY

Ivy is basically a simple plant, both a vine and a bush. But when space is limited, and you want a vertical statement, take advantage of its vining and give it all the support you can. This means trellising or a lattice framework. You achieve a screen, a background for flowering plants, an interruption in space, a subtle painting.

Hedera canariensis has shiny green leaves five to eight inches wide, with three to five shallow lobes. *Hedera canariensis variegata* grows better indoors, has irregular ivory marks which add patterning. It can clutch a wall in its eager trip upward, so a support form is needed to hold it away. It's rarely bushy and full, but is interesting behind the dark foliage of smaller plants. Put a pot on a pedestal so that the vine hangs and skinny space takes another direction.

Ivy needs light, lots of it, particularly in winter. Give it a cool, humid space, with less watering between October and March. Constant pinching back is part of a parent's job.

Red spider mite is a natural enemy. Misting and a thorough washing with a hose outside help keep away mites. Also, spray with Malathion solution if *that* doesn't send them up the wall.

Propagation: stem cuttings.

BAMBOO

Golden Cane bamboo, *Phyllostachys aurea,* can be grown in a tall narrow space indoors, provided that you understand it wants out in summer. If you are that rare plant parent who will live cool, be generous with fresh air and can find a bright diffused-light spot to spare, indoor living works the year around for bamboo. Most of us accept the cold facts and enjoy the lovely oriental beauty for as much time as it works mutually. P.S. When you move a bamboo, avoid sudden changes in light and temperature.

Phyllostachys nigra is a dramatic black-stem, an interior decorator's exclamation point. It's hard to find, harder to keep happy indoors. Plant people respect its royal lineage.

Bamboo grows slowly, stays in the same pot for years. Keep it out of sun or the leaf tips will burn. Keep potting mixture constantly moist; when leaves curl, it's thirsty. If you want to hold back growth, keep on dry side and don't feed. Otherwise, fertilize monthly spring to fall. Temperature range: 50° to 65°. Cut dead canes at root level.

Propagation: division of clumps.

IVY TREE

Except for the general shape of the leaves, *Fatshedera lizei* bears small resemblance to most common ivies. It grows more like a slender tree, not quite able to support itself but with a little help can dominate any skinny corner or window space. The stiff dark green leaves are dramatic, six to ten inches across, and highly polished.

You can train the stem when it is young and pliable, to any form which pleases. This type of ivy adapts better than the *Fatsia,* is less demanding than the oleander. Sun for four hours a day is fine; only don't let the hot midday glare cook it. Start its home in an east or west window. You'll know when the light level is too low because leaves drop. It will accept a wide temperature range from 40° to 72°.

Keep barely moist all the time, and allow three months between feedings. Prune back in February, and when you repot, it shouldn't be when new growth is pale green. Add sand and leaf mold to potting soil for vigor, drainage. Like the true ivies, *Fatshedera* is the unwitting host to red spider mites and black aphids. Don't let them get ahead of you; keep a sharp lookout when you water.

Propagation: stem cuttings in spring.

MALAYSIAN DRACAENA

Pleomele reflexa grows like the *Dracaena,* takes the same general care, but looks like you're seeing it through the wrong end of the binoculars. Its leaves are slightly twisted and about a third or a fourth of the size and length of the *Dracaena* clan's, and they grow close together on the stem so the whole plant looks like someone forgot it would shrink when washed. (Don't let that mislead you—*Pleomele* can eventually reach the 12-foot mark.)

Malaysian Dracaena is hardy, slow-growing and evergreen. Stems are supple. Three or more potted in a tall chromium-like mylar cylinder (with metal pot liner) makes terrific corner chemistry. Because the leaves turn this way and that, the plant is never monotonous, always giving a different face as the light moves.

Medium to bright light, average house temperatures and high humidity are the order of the day. Water just enough to keep the soil damp. *Pleomele* likes a tight girdle around its roots. Soil: one part peat, one part packaged soil.

Propagation: cuttings of growing tips, in spring.

PLANTS FOR SKINNY SPACES

MING ARALIA

Raising a Ming Aralia, *Polyscias fruiticosa,* is somehow like being parent to a Siamese cat. The Ming is elegant, aloof, and tends to do just what it wants to do, no matter how much love you deliver. In one location it will live diffidently for years, in another it will sulk and drop leaves—depending, of course, on the kind of attention you can afford to give. (It also drops a few leaves when moved, or when over-watered; takes several weeks to recover.)

The Ming, also called Parsley Panax, is a Polynesian relative of the *Aralia* family and grows to 40 feet in the tropics. It is a very slim plant with curling fern-like leaves on an irregular stem. One trunk looks skimpy and you need two or three to make a sculptural contribution.

Ming Aralia is sensitive to cold and to overwatering. Keep from drafts, in a warm protected area, and water weekly or when the top of the soil feels dry to the touch. It needs to be *barely moist,* and purrs when you apply misting. Use a pebble-filled saucer under the pot to step up humidity. Soil mixture: half peat, half packaged soil. Use pruning shears to "bonsai" the form. Bright indirect light seems to please. Feed every three months.

Propagation: stem cuttings.

OLEANDER

Why include a difficult plant when there are so many easy ones? Isn't a challenge more fun when you prove you can meet it? Oleander, *Nerium oleander,* is an outdoor, outgoing warm-weather baby from the Mediterranean. Only recently has it made the trip indoors, and being rather new at it, may be balky. Oleander grows wild in riverbeds which have dried up—its roots reach out for damp soil. So, in order to start out right, buy a five-gallon size and pot it up in a larger ceramic or wood tub where it can stretch its legs. Oleander has long thin stalks which grow almost straight up, and soft branches with grey-green leaves. The fragrant flowering comes in white, pink and red.

This plant is vigorous and evergreen provided it gets full sun and a good measure of bonemeal in the potting soil. Don't mist because it likes dry air. It is a chronic heavy drinker, from early spring to October; always take the chill off water before serving. Prune young side shoots to keep a narrow vertical shape. One problem: All parts of the plant are poisonous if taken internally—it's named for the poisons Nerein and Oleandrin.

Propagation: cuttings in water.

PARLOR PALM

Names can be confusing among the green things: *Chamaedorea adenopodus* is called the Parlor palm; so is *Neanthe bella*. The latter is a dwarf species usually found nestled in terrariums or small dish gardens. The one sketched here is a vertical clump with many canes sprouting to six feet after a slow start. Each stem has very bright green leaf pairs which mimic goldfish tails. *C. adenopodus* is unique among palms in that its fronds do not arch; each grows bamboo-straight.

Parlor palms were a Victorian passion, mainly because they could withstand temperature changes, miserable light, indifferent care—and still be beautiful. Not that *you* would consider neglecting this handsome palm. Give it the shadowless light of a north window or a curtained east one. Keep soil lightly moist and try a temperature range from 65° to 75° for its comfort. Parlor palms can stand a once-a-month feeding from April until September, then nothing during the winter. Repot only when there is no more room for stems, then proceed in March with a good packaged soil. Be sure the soil is firmed well around the old root ball.

PENCIL CACTUS

This strange creature comes from the desert side of Madagascar (there are two distinct climates in this neighbor of Africa: hot-dry and tropical-moist). *Euphorbia tirucalli* is only one of about 1600 species of the spurge family to migrate; its relatives include Crown of Thorns, poinsettia, and Devil's Backbone.

Pencil cactus is a succulent masquerading as a cactus, although it has no thorns. Most plant shops carry small *Euphorbia* but I suggest you look to a cacti specialist for an old plant, perhaps six or seven feet tall. The trunk is bald in the lower part, and the remaining weird branches are leafless stubs. Because it can be heavy, you may need large river stones to anchor the trunk in the soil.

Four or more hours of sun each day are needed by this contemporary living sculpture, and a temperature spread of 55° to 80°; a hot dry summer room is ideal. Roots need to be tightly confined, so repotting is rarely necessary. When handling, wear gloves because broken stems tend to bleed an irritating "milk"; keep it out of eyes and cuts. Stop the bleeding by squirting warm water on the plant's wound. Water weekly during summer.

Propagation: stem cuttings; let callus for five days before potting.

119

PLANTS FOR SKINNY SPACES

UMBRELLA PLANT

Cyperus alternifolius gracilis is a lofty semi-aquatic bog grass for warm rooms. Its silhouette and shadow pattern make good stage business. Rigid grass-like leaves spout like parasol ribs from the tips of tall three-angled stems. *Cyperus alternifolius,* Nile grass, is a smaller plant with soft umbrella leaves and is used in windowsill water gardens. Both are related to the ancient Egyptian plant, *Cyperus papyrus,* which grows six to ten feet tall and has thread-like leaves 18 inches long.

Umbrella plants should be potted in rich moist soil, one part peat, three parts packaged soil. Keep it in morning sun or semi-shade, with the temperature around 60° to 72°. About the water you use: If it is on the alkaline side, leaf tips will brown; neutralize tap water by adding a quarter ounce of ammonium sulphate per gallon. Standing the pot in a deep pebble saucer of water helps keep the soil properly dampened. Don't empty the saucer, just add more. Be free with misting.

Cyperus is such a distinguished plant, keep it groomed. Remove dead stems and blooms (pretty umbrella blossoms grow right out of the center of leaves); scissor off brown tips.

Propagation: by division.

YEW PINE

Podocarpus macrophyllus maki is dense, intense dark green, a column which takes fascinating twists as its spiral growth develops. It is a foil for a pride of lionizing shade-loving pots in front, plants with big leaves, plants with pale leaves. Take your pruning shears in February to keep its eccentric shape interesting. Chinese *Podocarpus,* another name for the Yew pine, grows to six feet indoors, and up to 40 feet in its natural habitat. Decorating note: Add tiny white Christmas lights any time of the year and you have your own special effects department. Hang it with mini-ornaments and you have a Yule tree.

If there's an outdoors to share, put the Yew pine out for three or four summer months, and bring it back in late August. It can tolerate some temperature fluctuations, but don't make a move until the weather is warm. Furnish filtered sunlight or semi-shade. Keep barely moist and mist on hot days. Feed in spring and fall. Needles yellowing? Try a little iron chelate. Pot in a large pot, and you won't have to repot for years. Add two tablespoons gardener's limestone to each gallon of soil (use half peat, half packaged soil).

Propagation: stem cuttings.

BAMBOO

Q *When one of the stalks of my bamboo dies what should I do?*

A This is not unusual indoors. You'll find signs of new shoots, too. Cut the dead *Phyllostachys aurea* cane at the root line. Leaving a stump is ugly, and also it may decay and endanger the plant. Trimming up the live canes to lift the foliage makes it a more interesting plant; cut the leaves as close to the cane as you can.

Q *My bamboo loses leaves when I bring it indoors after a summering on the deck.*

A Bamboo is sensitive to moves and a certain amount of leaf-fall is natural. A cool bright location indoors should reassure it you have its best interests at heart.

DRAGON TREE

Q *I have one Dragon tree, but it seems like it will never get to be the Dragon tree shape.*

A First, I would rush out and adopt at least two more *Dracaena marginata,* shorter than the one you own, and pot up all three in a bigger pot. Multi-stems seem to influence the Dragon to develop the contorted trunks. This is a "poodle" kind of plant. Skin up the trunks until there is a tuft at the end of each trunk. This shows the "bones" of the unusual stems.

FALSE ARALIA

Q *Why do the leaves of my False Aralia droop and get stiff?*

A Its present location may be lacking in humidity. *Dizygotheca elegantissima* should never really be allowed to dry out, and it needs misting several times a day in warm weather. It can't stand sunlight, either. Dry or soggy soil will cause leaves to drop.

MING ARALIA

Q *What are the little green bugs on the young shoots of my Ming Aralia?*

A Aphids, those soft-bodied insects which suck juices of the tender young leaves, making them stunted, curled up. Unless you get after them, they attract ants too. So take the Aralia outdoors, and spray it with a solution of soapy water; do this three weeks in a row, checking after each "laundering" to see if the aphids have been conquered. For a stronger soap solution, add a teaspoon of nicotine sulphate. Finally, a mild solution of Malathion should rout the hard-core holdouts.

MYRTLE

Q *I grow myrtle in my garden, but would like to try rearing a plant indoors which I can shear and make into a small topiary.*

A You can have your fun and make it work, too. Just find a cool sunny spot, a porch for your potted myrtle, and water when the soil is dry. *Myrtus communis microphylla* is a dwarf form, growing two to four feet tall, and has tiny fragrant bloom. Start shaping it when it is young, bending stems as well as "shearing" and holding the branches in shapes you want with fine copper wire, bonsai-fashion. Give it importance when you've got what you want by putting it on a pedestal in front of a narrow wall space which gets at least four hours of sun each day.

PLANTS FOR SKINNY SPACES

OLEANDER

Q *Why didn't the oleander have blossoms after I brought it inside?*

A You probably didn't prune back the oleander when it started its winter hibernation. Flowers grow on new wood. Also, its rest period starts in October and you may have to wait till next summer.

OREGON GRAPE

Q *I would like to keep the Oregon Grape by my front door but it is getting too big. Can I prune the sides and top?*

A You're a brave one to keep the *Mahonia lomariifolia* near a door. This is not a socially popular plant because its holly-like leaves will scratch like an unfriendly cat. Either the plant has to be moved—or you can try a drastic pruning by removing all the lower leaves and shaping a ball for the top of the stem. If there are several stems, skin them all up so that the remaining leaves are high enough to be avoided.

RUBBER TREE

Q *Could I trim a Rubber tree up like you suggested for the Oregon Grape? I wondered if it could look more like a tree?*

A Yes. I have a variegated *Ficus elastica* four and a half feet tall with just a large cluster of leaves at the top. Rubber plants eventually lose some of their lower leaves as they get older anyway. Skin up, or remove leaves which grow up the trunk of the Rubber plant to a point where it has formed branches. Look at the shape and do any side pruning which will turn it into a tree-top cluster. Protect floors from the milk which flows from cuts.

UMBRELLA PLANT

Q *Could I grow the Umbrella plant in my bathroom?*

A *Cyperus alternifolius* came from the swampy side of Madagascar and is ideal for bathrooms. Because of the fact that it likes morning sun or bright light, it could be a friend to take to a shower. It grows in water, so plant it in a sand-and-soilless-mixture pot. You don't empty out the existing water, just keep adding. Don't use hard water. Feed lightly once a week during spring and summer. Leaf tips brown if too much acid or alkaline content in the soil.

YEW PINE

Q *I've had a Podocarpus in a tub for several years, and the soil looks compacted. I live alone and repotting such a big plant is too much for me.*

A There are at least two ways to go: Check the yellow pages of your telephone book for gardeners, and hire one for two hours to do the replanting. The other way is to leave the plant in its present pot, scrape away as much of that compacted soil as you can without hurting the roots and replace with topdressing. (See section on repotting and top-dressing.)

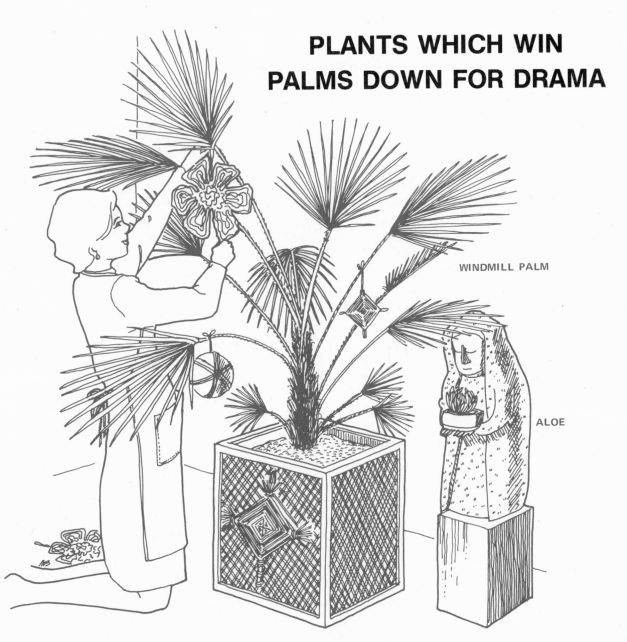

PLANTS WHICH WIN
PALMS DOWN FOR DRAMA

WINDMILL PALM

ALOE

PALMS FOR DRAMA

In Florida, near Cocoa Beach, the young Florida Institute of Technology has a campus. It was born of NASA engineers looking for ways to fill time between moon shots. One of these people happened to be a nut on palms—and he also happened to be one of the founders of the Institute. So, today, there are at least eight acres of palms, containing at least 300 species—and a more exciting walk-through I dare you to find. Winding paths bring new excitement at every turn. The collection is lovingly nursed by students who earn their keep this way. There are waterways to nurture moisture types; there are desert tribes in oasis conditions. There are great palms with leaves which never unfold, palms which grow huddled to the ground or Royals with 50-foot umbrellas.

See all these and you can understand the complete fascination with palms; their forms are magnets in any plant boutique. Even the smallest, miniature *Neanthe bella* which lives it up in terrariums, is a reverse binocular blast. Its tiny but perfect form is an elegant foil for the rest of the glass world it lives in.

The palms in this section are potentates of the plant world. You can find them as princely seedlings, but as young three-footers they hold court over any Steinway. A four-foot *Areca,* or Butterfly palm arches its delicate pale fronds like a ballet dancer—a star by the stair, a satellite behind the sofa. Give it authority and it will bestow favors.

Caryota, the mad Fishtail, is for the last of the big spenders. If you find yourself mesmerized by the superb form, by its romantic aura, you'll never be completely plant-happy without a Fishtail. (I can say this sorrowfully: Our modest four-foot slowly expired for no outward reason. Nematodes did it in, those little sneaks beneath the soil—the best reason I know for potting expensive plants in sterilized soil.)

The Fan palm is for big uncluttered spaces. Its height is about the same as its width. It has a sturdy dark trunk and those Cleopatranized fans. (For some reason, the Fan palm seems to be a perfect consort for a man's pad, surrounded by a collection of Greek statuary, Passion vines and an impeccable gourmet table.)

Lady palm, the *Rhapis,* can be a solitary beauty in a two-story space, a studio, a conference room. Nothing more is needed. The Date and the Windmill are bold, rewarding, too. Sago is the dwarf of these big ones—a baby to tempt people with offbeat taste. It is manageable size, wears well, one which gives its heart to Big Daddy. Once a cycad fancier, always, etc.

Palms like slightly acid soil, frequent summer watering and less in the winter. They don't seem to need a rest period like other greenery. Never let root balls dry out completely, and keep them out of direct sun and away from the blast of a hot air furnace. A good misting will discourage a common enemy: red spider mites. A dry warm palm is an invitation to the meanies—that includes scale and thrips, also. Never use an oil-base anti-bug spray; try an Ivory soap-and-water solution and spray the hairy trunk well where they may be infiltrating. Systemic chemicals hopefully work for advanced infections. A nicotine solution will eliminate fungus gnats on the soil. Rare plant specialist John Brudy says all palms are hooked on manganese sulphate, a fine white powder. Add a little each time you fertilize and see if you don't notice an upturn in their looks.

Big palms are for plant parents who will support all the way, with sacrifice, understanding and love. You may be in that select segment: check your palm.

In addition to the plants described on the following pages, other dramatic palms are: Chinese Fan, Bamboo, Parlor, *Chamaedorea elegans,* Dwarf Royal, Kentia.

PALMS FOR DRAMA

ARECA PALM

This superb formal palm has several proper names: Butterfly, Cane, Madagascar—depending on the whim of the plantsman who is trying to sell it. But no label can turn you on. You have to see the *Areca* and decide whether it fits your lifestyle, or you fit its. *Chrysalidocarpus lutescens,* or *Areca lutescens,* has very long arching delicate fronds which grow from a clump. The pale green leaflets are slim and feathery. The trunk is smooth except for the scars where leaves once grew.

Areca grows slowly, probably not more than six to ten inches a year. It summers outdoors nicely in a protected area where it can be shaded and spared from shredding winds. If your summer temperature drops below 65°, the palm must be indoors—or perhaps you might consider another species which won't need 75° to 80° days. Watering is very important. The soil should be damp at all times, but never let the pot sit in water. Feed monthly from March until September. Spider mite can be a sticky problem; wash the palm with sudsy water—don't use an oil spray. You can't prune an *Areca,* so if it outgrows your family, look for a foster home.

Propagation: seeds (slow).

DATE PALM

Sorry, a Date palm won't set you up in the date business—fruit only grows outdoors in warm climates —but it will keep guests occupied with conversation. *Phoenix canariensis* grows to 60 feet commercially, and so the nurseryman may try to switch you instead to *Phoenix roebelenii,* the miniature or Pygmy Date palm. But, if you have space, give the *canariensis* a whirl. Be bold. It's a great robust statement and worth moving out something else to make room.

Both species of *Phoenix* should be located in bright filtered sun; keep them well watered and misted, especially on hot days. They should also be potted up in soil which drains well. Give less moisture in winter months when the palm is resting. Feeding time is once a month. spring through summer. If you have a deck or a garden, shift the Date outdoors in the sun for a couple of months. It can take temperatures down in the 40's, but don't press your luck if the thermometer drops more.

Propagation: offsets or suckers from the bulbous base of the mother palm.

DWARF COCOS

This is perhaps the favorite house palm. The culture is easy but it is not likely to live to a ripe old age—it's sort of pre-elderly compared to the rest of the plants in this section. *Microcoelum weddellianum (Syagrus weddelliana)* is moderate in size, too, rarely reaching seven feet. You should find almost any size to start, from 12 inches up; a four-footer will be in a 12-inch pot.

Fronds of the Cocos are silvery green-blue, and the leaflets are rigid. The trunk is slim, with an overcoat of fibrous matting or hair. The plant retains its handsome form no matter how many leaves appear, but it can get as wide as it is tall.

Plenty of water is necessary; set the pot on a saucer filled with pebbles which are kept moist. Keep the temperature at least 65° in the winter. Top-dress the pot in spring (see detail, page 56). Cocos needs a deep tub and lime-oriented soil. Drafts cause tips to brown. If a leaf dies, cut it off right at the trunk.

Propagation: side shoots.

FAN PALM

The Fan isn't likely to outgrow its welcome. Three feet of plant in a large container seems friendly. Once in a while a six-footer comes along, but when you reckon it takes 30 to 50 years to get there, the three-figure price is not unreasonable for the care given all that time.

Chamaerops humilis is bushy, will have one main trunk and suckers at the base—a dense palm for screening something which you'd rather not see. Leaf stalks grow from the shaggy black trunk at different levels so the fans become an effective gray-green mass. Fans are at least 18 inches in each direction; they're stiff, pale and gray when they unfold. The stalks have spines not unlike the snout of a swordfish.

The Fan palm is not about to complain about temperature changes or lack of tender loving care. Half a day in sun or bright reflected light will do, but dark days won't send it into decline. Never, but never let it dry out. Spider mites and scale are less likely to attack a moist environment. Like the Cocos, it should be set on moist pebbles to increase the humidity. Temperatures can range from 55° to 72°. Pot in a mixture of one part packaged soil, one of peat. Feed monthly except October to February.

Propagation: seeds (slow), or suckers.

PALMS FOR DRAMA

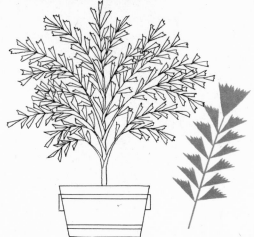

FISHTAIL PALM

Let me introduce you to the current "status" plant in decorating circles: *Caryota mitis,* the Fishtail. It's not unusual to see price tags from $350 to $600 for big ones, or about $50 per leaf. Of course, with a leaf 10 feet tall which took six months to develop, that's a lot of living green for the paper kind. Don't let this scare you, though. You can find a young plant in the $35 range which will do more for you than a *Ficus benjamina.*

Fishtail fronds continue to grow in size as they get older; eight to ten inches a year is not a lot so you won't have to start worrying right away about what you'll do when it threatens the people upstairs. Leaves are wildly cut; each section is fishtail shape. Two to four leaves on a young plant is average and when a new one appears, break out the champagne.

Give indirect light, the choice spot in the house, 65° to 75°, and always slightly moist soil. Don't let the tub sit in water. Feed in the spring and fall. Fishtail likes a tight-fitting pot but if you have to repot, choose a container only a couple of inches wider in diameter. Add good potting soil and two tablespoons bonemeal to each gallon of soil. P.S. You don't prune a *Caryota.*

LADY PALM

This slender bamboo-like palm was named many years before the Lib movement, but its elegant and vertical stance says: Never underestimate the power of a Lady palm. Don't ever downgrade this one because she'll end up queen of the scene. *Rhapis excelsa* is hardiest of all the palms. A hairy brown mat covers each thin stalk, and each stalk has very thin arching stems which grow horizontally and have arching fans. It is reedy, vigorous, tough. *Rhapis e. flabelliformis* has broader leaflets in each fan. *Rhapis humilis* is slender, smaller, and has been grown indoors for hundreds of years by the Chinese.

Lady palm does best in filtered light, with a temperature range of 50° to 72°. It requires moist soil but can stand the wet-to-almost-dry treatment. Potting should be done in looser African violet-type soil. Feed once every three months. Watch for scale. This dread enemy gets in the hairy covering of the stem and is almost impossible to lick. Try a systemic application to counteract.

Propagation: offsets which can be cut out with some roots attached.

SAGO PALM

This is one of my favorites because it is such a fascinating fraud: Sago is neither a palm nor a fern; it is related to the cone-bearing conifers, of all things. *Cycas revoluta* is among the oldest plants still alive. Its primitive form was present two hundred million years ago.

Sago is small compared to other palms, but it can hold the center stage with all the clout of a star. It is a sophisticated plant. If there's only that in your den, for example, the whole room is plant-furnished. Leaves with many narrow glossy leaflets, almost like a fern, appear out of an obvious and bulbous football shape, half buried. It is a slow grower. A two-foot height is easy to manage any place. But finding a four-foot specimen is rare and costly, and a 10-footer is probably only for a conservatory.

Sago does well with filtered bright light and a wet-to-dry watering. Feed every other month, March to August (never feed a newly potted palm but wait at least six months). It is practically indestructible, given spring and summer sun, but protect from hot days with shade and lots of misting. Yes, you can set it outside in summer.

Propagation: young shoots or suckers.

WINDMILL PALM

This is one of the larger palms, but in its pre-teen years it is an asset when you can't afford furniture and need an impressive space filler. Windmill, *Trachycarpus fortunei*, has large fan leaves up to two and a half feet wide which grow out of a bearded stout trunk. If you start with a young palm, it can continue living in that pot for several years if good light, adequate water and food are provided. The spiny leaf stems are not really deadly; they just look it. If the Windmill's spread threatens to take over the room, try tying it back with braided macrame ties.

Trim the lower fronds when they begin to show their age. If the top fronds look unhappy, it probably wants more light: Move the palm outdoors; then bring it back in before fall. Temperature range should be 50° to 75°. Keep the leaves washed to give them pollution-free living. Drainage is all-important; keep evenly moist. Cut back watering to half in winter.

Propagation: seeds (very slow); buy a young palm at a nursery.

PALMS FOR DRAMA

ARECA PALM

Q *How often should I repot a Butterfly palm?*

A When it's young, repot each spring. Older plants, when they're four feet tall, can wait two to three years. Use a deep narrow pot and be sure to firm the ground around the root ball, particularly at the edges. When repotting, do *not* put a small palm in a big pot; plant it in the next larger size. Palm soil should be a packaged mixture slightly on the acid side (pH 5 to 6.5). Never feed a dry palm, and withhold feeding a newly potted one for six months.

BAMBOO PALM

Q *The leaves on my Bamboo palm have a kind of yellow look and I'm worried.*

A Watering could be your problem—not enough. Dunk the whole pot in a tub of water so that it seeps all the way through; top-watering often doesn't find its way into a tight root ball. In winter this is not as important, but spring through fall you should lean on a good watering at least once a week.

DATE PALM

Q *My Date palm finally has some seeds. Could I try to make new plants?*

A Yes, but don't expect quick results. Plant the seeds in a mixture of soil, humus and sand. Keep moist, with a plastic cover over the top to hold in moisture, and keep the temperature at about 70°. Bottom heat will encourage seeds to sprout. This slow growth is why palms are expensive. It takes years to grow a palm to a marketable size, and someone has to be paid to watch over it all that time.

Q *Can I grow a Date palm in my office? There are big banks of fluorescent lights, on seven days a week.*

A You certainly should have success as long as the lights are lit on a regular basis. Miniature Date palms are most durable. Keep the soil moistened always.

FISHTAIL PALM

Q *I love the Fishtail palm but I can't afford it. Can I get seeds?*

A You can start a *Caryota* from seeds—if you are young! These palms take years and years to reach the expensive sizes. Why don't you see if you can find someone with a Fishtail which has suckers growing at the base and ask for a start? If you've been lucky and managed to get such a sucker, pot it up in a mixture of one part loam, one part sharp sand, one part peat and one-half part dried steer manure. To each gallon of this mix, add a couple tablespoons of bonemeal. Fishtail likes a tight pot condition so don't start your baby in too big a carriage.

KENTIA PALM

Q *When I took my Kentia palm out of its pot to put it in a bigger one, the roots were so matted I wonder if it will be set back by repotting?*

A A good-sized *Howeia* doesn't need a bigger pot because repotting may encourage it to outgrow your location. If you were to repot again, I would suggest removing the palm and some of the soil around the roots. Then, root-prune back about a quarter inch all around. Clean the pot thoroughly and disinfect it with a water/bleach solution. Then repot the palm adding new soil. Ram the new mixture firmly around the edges of the pot.

LADY PALM

Q *I think my Rhapis palm has scale, and it seems to get into the brown hairs on the stems. What can I do quickly?*

A The time to do battle with scale on a *Rhapis* is right in the beginning when you first notice a yellowing leaf. Yours sounds like it has an advanced case, and the only thing which may save the plant is to apply systemic spray or granules; the roots absorb this and then when the little sucking insects take in some of the poison in the plants juices, it zaps them. For a light problem, wash the plant with soapy water and spray with a solution of Malathion. Repeat at least three times to catch all the relatives.

NEANTHE BELLA

Q *How big will my Neanthe bella get? It is about a foot tall now.*

A *Neanthe bella* or *Chamaedorea elegans* comes from Mexico, is considered a dwarf palm, and rarely gets taller than four feet indoors. Eventually the stems will be about the diameter of a pencil and without spines on the edges. Full-size leaves are about seven inches long. You should have an "inflorescence" or pseudo blossom when the palm is young. The blossom eventually grows into a kind of non-edible fruit.

SAGO PALM

Q *Someone told me the Sago palm needs lots of water; is this true?*

A Not true; it needs to become partially dry between thorough waterings. Don't let the pot stand in water. If you double pot, check the holding pot; water has a way of accumulating. The safest way to be sure the plant's pot is not constantly wet is to put a layer of rocks or gravel in the larger one before putting the *Cycas* pot inside.

ANTS

Q *I have been bothered by tiny black ants in the house. Will they do damage to my palm?*

A The presence of ants on a plant is usually a sign that you have another problem: Scale and mealy bugs leave a sticky sweet residue and the ants make for that. Be sure to check your palm for these serious enemies, then put out ant repellent sticks or liquid.

FUNGUS GNATS

Q *Can you identify some little dark things like flies that hop around in the soil of my palm?*

A These are fungus gnats, and they lay their eggs in soil. The eggs hatch into threadlike maggots which attack the feeder roots. A nicotine sulphate solution or a Malathion solution poured through the soil kills eggs and maggots.

TEMPERATURE

Q *What's a good temperature for growing palms?*

A Minimum recommended is about 65°, but 55° won't put a strain on most palms. Avoid direct sunlight; give plenty of water during warm summer days, moderate the rest of the time. Misting will raise the humidity they like. Watch for spider mites during extended periods of warmth.

131

PLANTS TO BACK UP OTHER PLANTS

SPIDER PLANT
IN BAMBOO
BIRD CAGE

HOLLY
FERN

RICE PAPER PLANT

KALANCHOES

BROMELIADS

BEGONIAS

GREENHOUSE ROOM ADDED TO PATIO

If you have to slip into a combat jacket to keep from being listed as a "missing person" in your jungle of plants, you'll recognize the safety factor of having at least one large-foliage marker to bring you back alive. Every collection worth the space it wrenches from its owner needs a showpiece to lead the eye. For instance, with 50-plus pots in a bay window, some hanging, some on the floor, there should be one really large-leaf specimen to tie them all together. One specimen provides tranquility at the grass roots; a singular six-foot *Tupidanthus* is like an only child of older parents, in charge of his peers.

Are you really aware of the texture and shapes of your jungle residents? What does the addition of a new member do for old-timers? Will it frustrate or freshen the scene? Add a voluptuous-leaf winner and the mix of big leaves and small, of shades of green, meshes.

Most of us shop for indoor plants the way a husband indulges in impulse buying in a supermarket. Blindly choosing a plant to live with is to find yourself cohabiting with a pathologically insecure child. If you learn any lesson in the process of building a collection of greenstuff, it's that the way it looks in the nursery isn't the way it will look when you get it home because its new neighbors are different.

You will find you don't mix prickles (like the *Yucca*) with ice-creamy heliotrope. You don't put Bear's Breech next to an Elephant-Foot tree. You *will* find you can mix ferns and Roxburgh fig, or Castor Oil trees and a whole tribe of small-leaf greenies. What really counts is that mix of textures, with at least one great leaf plant to back up the rest of the family, provided they have the same growing needs.

Some of the plants listed in the section on Tall Folk & High Ceilings can be included in this search for a key back-up plant for a collection. The ones which follow in detail in this section are very special, assertive. Make a list and the next time you go plant-browsing, ask to see a *Clusia*, a *Ctenanthe* (buy it if you find it because they're hardy, but hard to find), a False Panax. Beauties like the Rice Paper plant are easy to come by, grown by nurseries for outdoor containers; Roxburgh fig may only be found in California and Florida, as will Sea Grape. The

133

BACK-UP PLANTS

latter can be started from seed; my seedlings are a year old and I'll have enough to furnish the neighborhood when they're weaned. As for the tree ferns, you'll have to decide how much *you* want to give up to generate the conditions they demand to live respectably indoors. Don't be impatient if you can't find some of these immediately. Just start a savings account and mark it "back-up." And when the right plant comes along, you'll know.

In addition to the plants on the following pages, other plants for back-up are: Bamboo palm, Snowflake tree, Chinese Fan palm, and Fingerleaf or *Philodendron selloum.* If you're looking for a tree form, the Little Leaf fig, the *Jacaranda* or the laurel will lift themselves above the jungle floor.

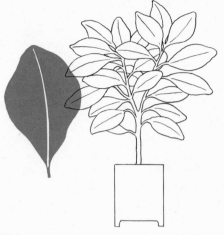

CASTOR OIL TREE

It's a pity that unpleasant recollections can get in the way of name association. But if you can't take the idea of a Castor Oil tree, just call it by its other name, Japanese aralia—and you've struck oil. *Fatsia japonica* has jumbo economy-size nine-lobed leaves, measuring 10 to 16 inches across. They are vigorous, shiny, and crown a tubbed plant five to eight feet tall and almost as wide. Careful pruning can keep size in hand and a cutback in February to open up the center helps its shape. Small white flowers appear on older plants, then develop into black non-edible berries. The *Fatsia* redistributes growing efforts if you pinch off blossoms.

The Castor Oil tree tolerates low light and cool 50° to 60° rooms if there's air movement. But good bright light and a cool enclosed porch or greenhouse is just what the doctor might order. Another thing: It is a heavier drinker than most. If over-heated or dry, it wilts; yellowing comes from sunburn. Feed monthly. Watch for scale and spider mites.

Propagation: suckers, from base of the *Fatsia*.

CLUSIA

There is more to a big house plant than meets the eye. The way the light dances on a shiny green leaf or shadows play on the wall behind—these things are what one feels as well as sees. What a magnificent plant like *Clusia rosea* does with light, shadow and form demonstrates this bonus. And it doubles the bonus by offering a dramatic background for fine foliage greens like Ming fern, Flowering Maple or a whole collection of begonias.

Clusia is a succulent evergreen tree and grows in the West Indies as a wild epiphytic on rocks, on other trees. Its fat, oval leathery leaves have no lateral veins; leaves grow in opposite pairs on hairy-brown branches. If the light level is too low, they start dropping. Large rosy flowers bloom on older plants.

Moderate light and cool dry atmosphere, around 65°, help growth; *Clusia* can stand up to 80°. Water to keep evenly moist but cut back the amount in winter to give plant a rest. A potting mixture of half peat, half packaged soil is recommended. Fertilize every other month, spring through fall.

Propagation: stem cuttings.

135

BACK-UP PLANTS

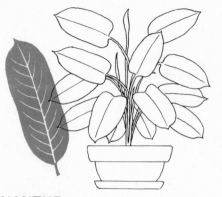

CTENANTHE

Ctenanthe tricolor is related to *Maranta* and *Calathea,* but, as in some families, there are a few members who gather great size while the rest stand by and watch. This perennial herb is grown for its great waxy, intense green leaves, 10 to 14 inches long, stiff and upright or at right angles to the ends of long stalks. Occasional white flowers are insignificant. Where the short relatives have peacock colors and decorative patternings, *Ctenanthe* has magnitude (three to four feet tall) and will command an open space. Find a very special container to match this personality: an old brass jardinière, brightened with much polish, or a copper cook pot from Turkey, or a Limoges cachepot. Place the *Ctenanthe* pot inside (with pebbles underneath to keep it from standing in water). The result is not Versailles, but it identifies you as a collector.

Filtered light, moister-than-most potting mix, warm temperature (65° to 85°), high humidity—they all contribute to *Ctenanthe* image. Soil content should be equal parts of leaf mold, builders' sand and potting soil to aid drainage. Mist on hot days.

Propagation: divide clump with a sharp knife.

FALSE PANAX

Pseudopanax lessonii is a member of the aralias and hails from New Zealand. It is an open attractive tree, sometimes with more than one stem, and with dark palmate leaves like *Schefflera,* only smaller and tougher. Leaves develop on horizontal stems on this tall, slim plant and do so in an interesting way—new foliage seems to break out of a plastic casing. This can sometimes deform a leaf but you can play pediatrician at the breech-birth with a pair of tweezers, gently pulling back the casing. Stems and even the trunk will show remains of these strange whitish casings for a long time (the condition has nothing to do with bugs or allergy). Branches will appear only on older plants.

False Panax wants bright light and air movement, but can't abide hot sun. Good drainage for an evenly moist soil and high humidity with misting will do the job. Don't let it dry out; leaf stems will turn brown at the trunk and drop. Overwatering will also cause this. Feed monthly spring and summer with half-strength fertilizer. Misting discourages spider mites.

Propagation: stem cuttings.

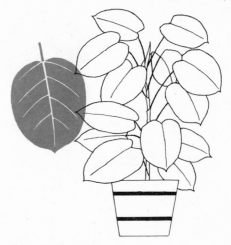

RICE PAPER PLANT

Rice Paper plant is another great-leaf marvel to expand your mind—and do your meditating under. *Tetrapanax papyriferus* has deeply lobed leaves one to two feet wide on long furry stems, with the same furry felt on the undersides. Growing multi-stemmed, it spreads as wide as it is high, and that can be five to six feet. Trunks lean out gracefully so it becomes an architectural space-maker. Clusters of pale cream flowers may appear on furry stems in winter.

Rice paper, the lovely sheer material used in Japanese shoji screens, is made from the white tissue in the stems. It first appeared in Chinese scrolls, with drawings of plants and animals, and was also used to make artificial flowers.

Turn on the sun for *Tetrapanax* (also identified as *Aralia papyrifera*), but shield from hot midsummer midsummer light, as they sunburn. Rice Paper plant has a deep root system, and should have a big container. Digging around the base of the plant with an old fork can stimulate growth of suckers for new plants. Use a good packaged potting soil and keep it on the moist side. Temperature can range from 50° to 72°. Feed in May and August.

ROXBURGH FIG

Ficus roxburghi is strictly for the adventurous and the bold. It is the Mercedes of the fig family: When you first gaze on its impressive 14- to 16-inch leaves and understated structure, you'll understand that its owner can stand being labeled a plant chauvinist. Yet Roxburgh's ample bulk does not distract from a group of smaller-leaf figs, like the Weeping fig or the variegated Rubber plant. In fact, it is a subtle foil for cut-leaf greens like *Fatsia japonica* and *Philodendron selloum.* The young Roxburgh leaves are maroon when they appear, and later become rich dark green.

Care and feeding are about the same as for the other figs: bright light or reflected, and full winter sun, plus temperature range from 65° to 75°. High humidity and ventilation are musts. Set the container on a pebble tray and check to be sure the drainage is working properly. Mist a couple times daily when the thermometer goes above 72°. Feed monthly after it is acclimated. If there's leaf-dropping, it's trying to tell you the location is too cool or too hot.

Propagation: cuttings in spring.

BACK-UP PLANTS

SEA GRAPE

Sea Grape really turns me on as the tall, dark, rich plant in the crystal ball! Sea Grape, *Coccoloba uvifera* is the most memorable tree in Florida (that's where I got seeds to start mine, from that master rare-seedsman, John Brudy—see list of sources, page 32). There they are planted in the median strips of highways, they grow wild in the dunes at the ocean, they become accent trees for inner courts, pools.

Waxy leaves are large five- to eight-inch saucers, olive-green and tough like dry leather, with bronze undersides and heavy veins—likely to turn brilliant oranges and reds when they age. Flexing branches make it possible to prune and maneuver bonsai contours. Bonus: delicious purple grapes which follow white blossoms when grown in ideal conditions. Furnish lots of sun and warmth and you will reap the delicious jelly from their juice.

Sea Grape is a robust plant once it gets growing. It can live indoors in bright light but prefers sun, with warm days and cool nights. During winter months, keep cool and drier so it can rest; the balance of the year, evenly moist but not constantly wet. Add coarse builders' sand to the potting mix.

Propagation: seeds (50 to 100 days to germinate.)

TUPIDANTHUS

If you like the *Schefflera,* you'll love the *Tupidanthus,* to paraphrase a cliché. The former is a favorite in a small pot and full grown at seven feet, easily available and sturdy. But *Tupidanthus calyptratus* is another tall game. Its leaves are darker, richer and its reddish stems and trunk are sturdier than the schefflera's. It is only just coming into its own as a super plant for big spaces. As with anything new and difficult to locate the price tag may be more than one on a schefflera same size, but as a specimen, *Tupidanthus* is the more commanding, entrancing.

Loose soil and very good drainage are important. My six-footer is planted in half wood shavings and half potting mix, and the water goes right through. This means more frequent checking so it isn't overwatered and care that the container doesn't sit in a wet saucer. Warmth and filtered light are required. Keep leaves shiny by regular damp-dusting. *Tupidanthus* is more resistant to pests than most big-leaf greenery, and less prone to leaf-drop, keeping most of its bottom leaves.

Propagation: cuttings.

TREE FERNS

These four tree ferns have been mustered here because they have two things in common: They're all focal-point beauties for big uncluttered spaces, plants which are romantic, airy, lush—and they're all difficult to keep happy indoors!

Tree ferns take to greenhouse living, with plenty of cool moist air, no direct sunlight (except in midwinter). But, bring them indoors and you have a challenge: Place one under a skylight, by an enclosed swimming pool, in a glass garden room, in a greenhouse wing off the kitchen. Like raising a child genius, if it was easy anyone could do it.

When you finally put the fern in place, give it two weeks of intensive misting care (twice a day). Be sure the watering you do is going into the root ball. It's worth getting a water wand, a kind of probe which forces water directly into the roots. A pebble tray helps keep a moist atmosphere; a layer of pebbles on top of the soil holds in dampness. Feed monthly May to September. If the growing tips wilt, the fern needs immediate watering.

Propagation: spores, at any season.

AUSTRALIAN TREE FERN: *Alsophila cooperi* has delicate arching fronds; tree grows to eight feet. Plant in firbark, sand and leaf mold mix. Never mist so late it goes to bed with a wet head. Can be moved to a shaded garden spot in summer, but hose-mist it on warm days. A 50° to 70° range is agreeable.

HAWAIIAN TREE FERN: *Cibotium glaucum* has feathery gold-green leaves in a spreading crown, leaving openness under the tree. Keep warm, moist and bathed in high humidity; wants indirect light. Get a trunk from Hawaii, keep warm and damp to grow. *Cibotium schiedei* is the Mexican cousin.

NEW CALEDONIA TREE FERN: *Blechnum gibbum* has a slender trunk three feet high with spreading crown of stiff symmetrical growth. Give shade, moist soil. Avoid overhead watering; it doesn't need humidity like the others. *Blechnum* is one fern which will thrive in an apartment, out of sunlight.

JAMAICAN TREE FERN: *Cyathea arborea* spreads like a patio umbrella with its tall single trunk and flat stiff fronds; they are more like the woodsy fern shape. Bright indirect light is called for again, a warmth range of 50° to 70°, and potting mix which is half-and-half peat and package soil.

139

BACK-UP PLANTS

CASTOR OIL TREE

Q *Why do the edges of my Castor Oil tree leaves look sunburned? It gets some sun and is in front of a cool white wall.*

A *Fatsia japonica* does better in bright light than sun, and your "cool" white wall may be reflecting hot sunlight. If you can't change the wall color, move the plant. Check temperatures during the day to keep *Fatsia* cooler than 65°. Pruning older plants in spring gets rid of unsightly leaves and encourages vigorous new growth.

CTENANTHE

Q *I bought a big-leaf plant and was told it is a Bamburanta. When I went to the Arboretum I saw one and it was labeled Ctenanthe; which is right? Can I make cuttings?*

A You and the Arboretum are both right: *Ctenanthe compressa* is often sold as *Bamburanta,* and *C. oppenheimiana* is named Giant Bamburanta. This is because this plant is a relative of the *Maranta,* and has a bamboo look. Cuttings will root in water. If you're repotting, I'd recommend dividing the root clump.

FALSE PANAX

Q *My False Panax is just the right size for the location where I put it and I don't want it to grow taller. If I cut off the top, will it kill the plant?*

A You may cut the top or air layer it to make another plant. Any removal of a plant's top causes it to put forth more growth at the sides. Also, confining the roots holds back growth, so don't repot for at least a couple of years.

INDIA LAUREL

Q *I have a Ficus nitida tree which has been doing well in my kitchen greenhouse. Now the leaves seem to fall more and more. What would cause this?*

A India Laurel, or Little Leaf Fig, seems to be susceptible to thrips, and this is tough to control. If the leaves are curled and stippled, thrips are your trouble. Spray the tree with a good soapy water solution, and move the tree outside to give a Malathion treatment, as a last resort.

ROXBURGH FIG

Q *I have been growing a Roxburgh fig on a deck off my living room, and I bring it in each winter because our climate is cold. It has some small bumps on the stems now. Is something wrong with the plant?*

A More likely the fig is "expecting": Roxburgh will get a crop of figs in its older age. They usually come in clumps on the trunk and branches.

RUSTYLEAF FIG

Q *Recently, I ran across a Ficus I'd never seen before. I think it is called Rustyleaf. Can you tell me anything about it?*

A That would be *Ficus rubiginosa,* and it has become available only recently in plant centers. Its leaves are five-inch ovals; Rustyleaf grows single and multiple trunks. It will grow tall, raise easily like other members of the *Ficus* family, and take warmth. The distinguishing leaves are dark green on top, and rusty-wooly underneath.

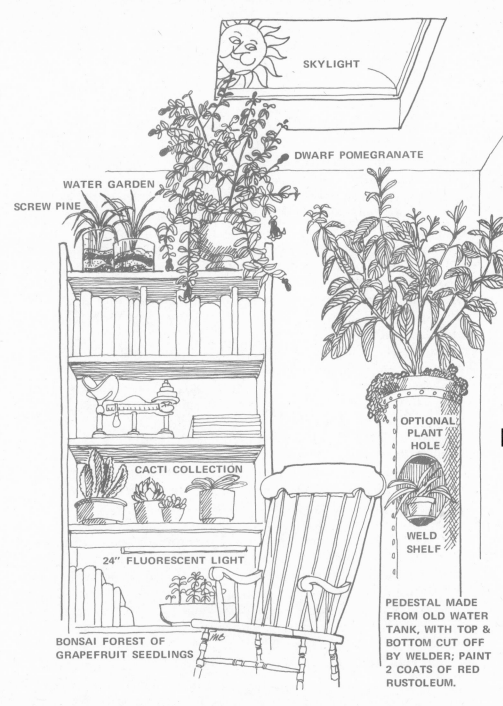

SKYLIGHT

DWARF POMEGRANATE

WATER GARDEN

SCREW PINE

CACTI COLLECTION

24" FLUORESCENT LIGHT

BONSAI FOREST OF
GRAPEFRUIT SEEDLINGS

OPTIONAL
PLANT
HOLE

WELD
SHELF

PEDESTAL MADE
FROM OLD WATER
TANK, WITH TOP &
BOTTOM CUT OFF
BY WELDER; PAINT
2 COATS OF RED
RUSTOLEUM.

PLANTS THAT BEAR FRUIT UNDER SKYLIGHTS

PLANTS THAT BEAR FRUIT

So you don't have a skylight. Perhaps it has never occurred to you to consider how beneficial a window in a roof can be. On a rainy day, you look up and watch the drops explode; when it's sunny you are bathed in good vibes. I once lived in a house with seven skylights, each about two feet square, and I can vouch for the wonderful things they did to the inside of that house. You wouldn't believe the enchantment of moonlight checkering the floor below.

I have a 30-inch square in my kitchen now, and the *Clerodendrum* on a shelf below bathes every morning in the sun and has had 40 blossoms this month. For about $150 you might be able to install a modest plastic pre-fab skylight unit, depending on your roof condition, codes and source of supply. Perhaps this is a fresh thought in regard to your plant children.

Fruit trees can be grown indoors without a skylight; in fact, most indoor plants succeed with side-direct, reflected, filtered or not-so-hot light, depending on their needs. But there's only a remote chance a fruit tree will flower unless you furnish overhead sun. There *is* reassurance of a harvest if the tree's light needs are met.

Another plus: Fruit trees grown indoors can be trained as espaliers as well as developing into tree shapes. That is, you build a frame to which the young tree is shaped and tied, and instead of growing in all directions, it becomes two-dimensional, or a flat form. Put the frame and container on wheels, and you have a living movable screen. You can also move the tree so that it gets maximum sun.

In France, pears are grown in espalier forms for commercial consumption. The rows are just far enough apart for a picker to load his basket, and the height of the espalier is controlled so no ladders are needed. There is extra labor in pruning and shaping, but the resulting crop is worth it. (The canny French also came up with that great idea of growing a pear in a bottle, and with the addition of some *eau de vie,* produced a delicious liqueur. When the first sign of the young fruit shows, it and the branch are slipped through the neck of the bottle and carefully tied so that the fruit matures right in the glass. I wonder if anyone has ever tried that trick indoors.)

The most difficult fruit trees to raise indoors are the citrus. They need soil on the acid side and an extra boost of iron when the leaves get jaundiced. Watch for spider mite if there's a dullness on the top of the leaves, and a general blotchy sickness. Spray with a solution of soapy water, and follow up with at least three separate sprayings of a Malathion solution. However, if there is fruit on the tree, keep on with the weekly soapy bath, and hose down regularly until the tree revives. Because of this problem, it is a smart idea to put wheels under a citrus so you can move it outdoors and back without strain.

There are many unusual fruits which may be started from seeds. These include *Carambola,* mango, St. John's Bread, cocona, Sea Grape, lychee, Passion fruit, and on and on, including even the over-planted avocado!

In addition to the plants described on the following pages, other plants that bear fruit under skylights are: Natal plum *(Carissa),* kumquat *(Fortunella),* dwarf pomegranate, dwarf banana, South American tomato *(Cyphomandra betacea),* runnerless strawberries—and tea *(Thea sinensis).* Look for limequat, tangelo and citron, too.

PLANTS THAT BEAR FRUIT

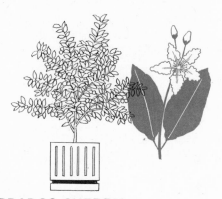

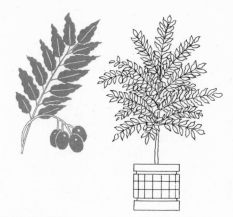

BARBADOS CHERRY

A handsome bush masquerading as holly, but with cherry-size fruit you can brew up into ambrosial jams, and a sauce to inspire vanilla ice cream. *Malpighia glabra* takes its time about growing up, but it begins to show flat blush-red blossoms with shaggy edges, size of a nickel, when it is still a four-inch baby. Color appears in summer, and by fall begins to show pie-cherry shape red fruit. This pretty fruit is on the acid side, has a thin skin, and a large four-angle seed which means you can start more plants for special friends.

Leaves are prickly like holly, and elliptical. Young branches can be cut back to imitate a bonsai; Barbados cherry can be kept a compact size so that it can be put in any number of places where you need a single decorative plant. It blooms its head off with half a day's sun, but will be your friend with good exposure to bright light or partial shade. Keep the soil on a moist-to-almost-dry pattern, and feed early spring and summer, every other week. Humidity should be in moderate range.

Propagation: seeds, cuttings.

KAFFIR PLUM

Harpephyllum caffrum, by way of South Africa, could be a twin of the Coffee tree, they're so much alike in looks. Both grow with a single straight trunk, with similar crinkled and shiny dark leaves. The plum's new leaves unfold as red and slowly turn green-black. I do mean slowly—it demands the patience of a mother. But when the clusters of white or greenish small flowers appear, the fruit will finally be not too far behind.

It's a handsome little tree, an evergreen, and can be trained to a striking silhouette by careful pruning. An old plant has hard heavy wood, and deserves a very special container to give it proper importance. The fruit is dark red, size of an olive, thin-skinned and pulpy. It's tart but not unpleasant to nibble on. Don't count on enough for a Viennese plum torte for the first year's crop.

Kaffir plum takes heat, sun, and dotes on good ventilation. A daily misting is a good idea in warm periods. Fertilize every month from March to July. Water as for Barbados cherry.

Propagation: seeds, cuttings.

LOQUAT

Loquat is the showpiece tree for your experiment in growing fruit indoors. It can get to be 10 feet tall, with leaves grander than the rest of the fruit trees, and its crop more than you can handle once it starts bearing. All the loquat asks is an overhead skylight or a large south-facing glass window wall—and stand aside! If you start the tree young enough, it can be espaliered against a white wall on a trellis to get maximum reflected light. Look for grafted varieties like Champagne and Gold Nugget.

Eriobotrya japonica comes from the Orient, and in California it is a favorite patio tree, either in the ground or in a tub. The leaves are almost a foot long, glossy deep green with rust "wool" on the underside. New branches are somewhat wooly, too. Small white flowers in clusters add good smells to the house, and the one- to two-inch orange-yellow fruit is aromatic. The pulp is tart but delicious.

Loquat needs lots of moisture, weekly feeding in spring and drainage. Cool it in winter. Prune back to let light into the center leaves; if there's too much fruit, remove some so the others will get larger.

MEYER LEMON

Citrus limonia meyeri is an old friend in California gardens, where it is treated as a fragrant ornamental shrub. Well, it does nicely indoors, too. It's a proper size for studio apartments, mobile homes and condominiums, and its living habits will fit in with most people on the move. When you buy a Meyer lemon, look for one budded or in bloom because they mature earlier.

Meyer lemon is rounder, deeper yellow than the grocery store variety. It is not as tart but has a tangy aroma and a thin rind which is excellent grated into a cream pie. *Citrus limonia ponderosa,* Ponderosa lemon, also puts out an edible but bland lemon, but its huge size dwarfs the tree—up to two and a half pounds for a single lemon.

Prune to keep the shape which looks best in the space the lemon lives. Keep in mind that you may have to make like a bee and do a cross-pollination to get fruit. Lemons need heavy summer watering, better-than-average drainage. And most of all, turn on the sun. Watch for spider mites; if infected take the tree outdoors and spray with soapy water (no detergent). Misting discourages an invastion.

Propagation: from seeds, and half-ripe wood cuttings, spring.

145

PLANTS THAT BEAR FRUIT

PERSIAN LIME

This lime and the Meyer lemon are similar in growing needs and form, except that the lime stays bright chartreuse when ripe. The tree is more a bush and does well to reach two feet tall, but size doesn't inhibit its prolific crop. Again, buy grafted stock.

Citrus aurantifolia should have high humidity; check every day during hot weather for watering needs. Check to assure fast drainage, also. Overhead sun from a skylight or clerestory windows and summer warmth are in order. Acid soil and a feeding once a month from March to September will get you a healthy plant. However, don't overfeed, hoping to get more fruit; the result is that new leaves push off the tiny undeveloped fruit (this applies to all citrus).

The lime likes air movement and doesn't mind air conditioning. In winter hold back heavy watering and keep cool. Never let it dry out. Prune in spring to let light into the center of the bush, but watch your hands—the thorns are stinkers. Like the lemon it needs a high level of iron to keep leaves sharp green. Use chelated iron, or iron sulphate, available at garden centers.

PINEAPPLE GUAVA

Feijoa sellowiana grows high, wide and handsome in the garden, but with parental guidance should make an attractive teenager indoors. Pinching back the new shoots, together with judicious pruning in spring, should let it know who's giving orders.

Guava has beautiful white cup-shape flowers with red stamens. Pollination by hand is indicated in order to get a crop. Petals are edible, an exotic addition to a summer salad or as a garnish; the oval fruit is dull green and slight crimson flushed, and the soft pulp inside mimics pineapple in flavor. Leaves are dark green with a white midrib, and underside is covered with gray fuzz.

Two to four hours of sun would be ideal for the Pineapple guava, but a bright light, particularly if it bounces off a white wall, is still adequate. Temperature should range from a low of 50° at night to 70° days: if it turns hot, mist a couple of times a day. Give it good air movement and feed every other month starting in March.

Propagation: seeds, cuttings.

SURINAM CHERRY

In Brazil the *Eugenia uniflora* is called Pitanga; in Cuba, it's the Cayenne cherry. (In Brazil, the leaves are tossed across the floor and trampled so the odor will keep flies away.) In both countries, and in our gardens, it is trained as an espalier, on some sort of designed support. This is a neat idea for growing indoors, too; instead of just another tree you have a screen to divide two areas. Put the container on wheels and it can close off a kitchen from the guests, it can move to a bay window, it can bask in the noonday sun under a skylight.

Pleasantly pungent green leaves are bronze when young; branches are thin and flexible, easily bent to a frame. Fruit is deep crimson, smaller than a cherry tomato; its spicy acid flavor transforms jellies, sherbets into ambrosial concoctions.

Water heavily in summer, moderately in winter.

Propagation: seeds which germinate in about four weeks; repot when seedlings are 12 inches tall.

TANGERINE (MANDARIN ORANGE)

Knobby stockings filled with nuts, oranges (and a traditional hunk of coal in the toe!) hanging by the fireplace—every tangerine since childhood has tasted like Christmas. Now picture this tangy fruit on a tree **147** instead of in a sock, where Santa can help himself as he passes by annually.

Tangerines or Mandarins, Satsuma oranges *(Citrus reticulata),* Otaheites *(Citrus taitensis),* Calamondins (*Citrus mitis,* with one-inch, juicy-sour oranges), Seville sour oranges *(Citrus aurantium)*—they're all adaptable to skylight-living. There are also dwarf varieties developed by horticulturists. These seem to do exceptionally well as indoor trees.

All these varieties need as much sun as possible, thorough watering (but not left soggy, please), and feeding of a high-nitrogen fertilizer in March, June and August. Air movement is needed to keep the temperature near 68°; too concentrated heat is drying. Use the mister on hot days. Winter brings a need for cutting back on warmth, watering until February, but don't let them dry out. Pushing the plant outdoors in summer gives it an extra boost. Don't be surprised if it sheds some leaves on the return trip: keep your—and its—cool.

Propagation: seeds (plants from seeds rarely produce flowers); cuttings.

PLANTS THAT BEAR FRUIT

BARBADOS CHERRY

Q *My skylight opens for ventilation. Will this hurt the Barbados cherry?*

A *Malpighia* bears a charmed life with good ventilation, an open window or a vented skylight. If you can put it outdoors for part of the summer, it will enjoy gentle breezes and sudden summer rains. Good drainage is essential; this cherry likes watering on a very-wet-to-dry cycle.

DWARF BANANA

Q *There are some little plants at the base of my dwarf banana. Can these be removed and planted?*

A The plants are called suckers, and can be cut away from the parent plant without harming either. When you cut, use a sterilized knife and be sure to get some roots with the sucker. Pot it up in a mixture of packaged soil and sand. The dwarf banana, *Musa cavendishii,* will give some fruit in its third or fourth year. Give it winter sun, summer shade. Underwatering is better than overwatering.

GRAPEFRUIT

Q *Can I grow grapefruit from seeds of fruit I ate?*

A Yes, but don't expect to get a fruit-bearing tree; fruit trees started from seeds rarely bear fruit. Growing grapefruit treelets can be good fun, though: dry the seeds for about 48 hours, soak in lukewarm water overnight, and plant one-half inch below top of soil in a small pot. Cover pot with plastic food wrap, and put in a warm spot. Seeds should start sprouting in seven to ten days.

KAFFIR PLUM

Q *Will I get fruit on my Kaffir plum? I started it from a seed.*

A Trees like the *Harpephyllum* rarely have fruit when you start them from seed. Your best bet is to buy a young plant and nurture its fast growth. Grafting-on stock is final insurance of a productive life. That absence of fruit does not make the Kaffir less attractive; it is a handsome green form and a good addition to any collection.

LIMEQUAT

Q *What is a Limequat?*

A It's a cross between a Mexican lime and kumquat. Tangelo is a cross-breed result of tangerine and grapefruit getting together. These citrus extractions all need the same type of growing conditions: a slightly acid soil, fast drainage, moderate 65° to 72° days and cool nights, misting in warm weather.

LOQUAT

Q *What makes leaves of a loquat shrivel and dry?*

A Drainage is extremely important in a loquat's life. The fine hair-like fibrous roots must be kept evenly moist yet never heavy with water. Any unhappiness downstairs and the leaves will shrivel quickly.

NATAL PLUM

Q *Would you recommend putting the Carissa out-doors in the summer?*

A Natal plum is another fruit which benefits from an outing. Yes, put it in sun and where it gets ventilation so it won't overheat. Hose the plant down daily in hot weather; as well as being beneficial to the leaves, a hosing discourages problems like scale. The fruit of the *Carissa* is bitter but challenging, and stays on the bushy shrub for at least four months. Watering is the same as for Barbados cherry. *Carissa* is a fast grower, lends its two- to three-foot growth the first year to an espalier form.

PERSIAN LIME

Q *What causes leaf-drop on a Persian lime?*

A If the drop is in the winter months, this is a normal action. Any other time, it is possible that the drainage is poor and you're faced with root rot, probably terminal.

PINEAPPLE GUAVA

Q *Does the Pineapple guava need lots of water?*

A Give it a thorough drenching, then let it get dry to a depth of at least two inches before watering again. *Feijoa* responds to fresh air and a twice-daily misting in hot weather. Fruit ripens about five months after flowering, provided you furnished cross-pollination. Best pruning time would be spring before the blossoms begin to form.

TANGERINE

Q *My tangerine has something sticky on the leaves.*

A Aphids and scale will drop a sticky substance when they suck. I would spray the leaves with a soapy solution, hose it off outside after; repeat this washing at least three times in one month. Apply a systemic treatment to the roots as a final action. A daily misting in summer will help keep the bugs away.

Q *I tried eating the Calamondin orange but it was too bitter. I was told this is a good fruit and I'm disappointed because I hate to throw away the crop.*

A It *is* a good fruit—only this citrus should be concocted into a marmalade.

149

Q *How do I repot an orange?*

A Knock the plant out of its container onto a newspaper or a protective covering, and remove as much soil as you can. Wash off the rest under tepid water, and put it in a cleaned pot after you have done any necessary root pruning. (Remember, when you prune the roots of a plant you must also cut back top growth because it will lose more water than the cut-back roots can replace.) Add high-nitrogen fertilizer and chelated iron in the soil mixture, water and keep in a low-light condition for about two weeks. All citrus like cool nights, moderate days. Too much water and leaves get yellow blotches between the dark veins. However, never let any citrus dry out.

PLANTS THAT TURN ON FOR LIGHTS

This is a good place to spotlight and debunk an old gardening tale: There is no reason to grow indoor plants if one has a garden. Ha! That's one notion to toss into the trash bag. All those outdoor gardeners have to do is to rub the indoor fluorescent lamp, and out will jump 40 watts of genii to conjure seeds right out of their skins, faster, healthier and more prolific than garden-started seeds, and blossoms which last longer.

They find that seeds started in flats and kept warm with cables underneath have a sure start under man-made lights. Primroses started in January will bloom in spring, with larger-than-life blossoms; perennials seeded in the fall can spend the winter under lights, and then be planted out with greater success when the weather warms up outside. They discover that seedlings can be transferred to flats and held until final planting is scheduled. They find that plants started in a basement or cellar during the late winter develop stronger root systems.

And they have to acknowledge that the major share of indoor plants flourish with the help of fluorescents, and bloomers burst their genes. Greenery grows large and will spread more luxuriantly under lights. And the old, cold frames outdoors become holding areas rather than spring starters. Suddenly, the stubborn gardener becomes a sorcerer's apprentice, hooked on indoor planting, all because of those 40-watt genii.

Plants which normally opt for greenhousing live happily ever after in a winter vacation under lights and a summer outside in moderate climates. Orchids and bromeliads are particularly pleased with this life. *Epidendrum, Crossandra, Primula,* Crape Myrtlette, the gesneriads like *Streptocarpus,* African violets and *Gloxinia* respond to wintering in your cellar Florida. Annuals perform compatibly under artificial light. They're heavy sun soakers, but additional time under steady fluorescents seems to suit better than natural light.

For the handicapped, the senior citizens in wheelchairs, light gardening has reopened options for enjoyment of watching and caring for growing plants. Construction of a U-shape table, open below so that the chair arms will fit under the top, makes it possible to garden intensively under lights. Seed propagation, rooting of cuttings, building of tiny "trough" gardens, building collections of flowering species are among the unlimited possibilities.

Indoor lighting works in greenhouses, too. Mini-houses which come K.D. (knocked down, or you-put-it-together) can be set up in the garden, on a deck or a patio. Lights can be added over benches, with extra timing to make up for cloudy spring days. A four- by six-foot model with hinged door sells for about $125.

For the gardener without a garden, a cellar or a greenhouse, fluorescent fixtures can be fitted into closets, cupboards, under coffee tables, even in an unused fireplace. Units come in two-, three-, four-, six- or eight-foot lengths. Two 40-watt tubes, in pair, will adequately light a 12-inch-wide shelf below. For flowering plants, the space between should be less than 16 inches. Light intensity minimizes the further it gets from the foliage. Ceiling lights in an office will keep plants alive, but furnish little growth help. Leaving lights on longer makes up for some of the lower intensity.

Experts say that a warm-white and a cool-white together make an ideal combination. Investigate special plant lights too. Individual bulbs take ceramic sockets—don't try them in an ordinary lamp holder. You'll find that adding an automatic timer gives controlled light exposure, and relieves you of remembering.

Plants under lights do best in a soilless mixture. This is a combination of peat, vermiculite and perlite which you buy at nurseries. It's clean, light, and provides important drainage. Misting of foliage is important to keep high humidity and to discourage bug colonization. Organic food like fish emulsion gives a satisfactory diet.

In addition to the plants described on the following pages, other plants for indoor lights are: *Cuphea*, geraniums, miniature roses, *Aphelandra*, begonia, *Coleus*, *Dipladenia*, *Fuchsia*, *Impatiens*, *Ixora*, *Lantana*, *Lobelia*, dwarf pomegranate.

BROWALLIA

Intense blue-bell flowers cascade out of a white basket—months and months of bloom—all because of the witchery of man-made suns. *Browallia speciosa* is a 12- to 15-inch shrub which is treated as an annual, but with pruning it may come back for another blooming surprise. It is one of those happy plants which outdoes itself, beaming under lights or in a sunny window. Moderate heat is fine, but in summer move it farther away from overhead lights to filtered sunlight.

Browallia is a likely plant for a shelf or as a hanging basket. If you get converted by what a couple of 48-inch tube lights can do for your life, pot up four or six *Browallia* from seeds you start under the lights—and in no time, the whole room where they live will seem to ring blue bells. A dwarf variety may be on the market soon, "Blue Troll," with year-round blooming.

Normal watering is called for; don't let it dry out. Mist when air is dry or hot. It likes shaded roots. If it gets too hot, foliage turns red. Watch for white fly.

Propagation: seeds.

EPIDENDRUM

Bright star of the orchid family, *Epidendrum* responds like an angelic child to fluorescents. It is a compact plant, dainty in scale, with as many as a hundred miniature orchids on long reed-like stems eight inches to two feet long. Each individual blossom is the size of a yellow jacket, in the same brilliant yellow and orange, and with exquisite fringed lip. There are innumerable hybrids—pink, red, lavender and white as well as the yellow-orange.

Epidendrum is an easy terrestrial orchid, and seems to mutualize, as they say in advertising dialect, with family life indoors. Fluorescent tubes, placed about six inches from the plant, have tested out positively. All reed-stemmed *Epidendrum* need as much light as they can get, but want cool roots. Those with hard round pseudobulbs need a rest period in a quieter, darker spot; soft-leaf ones with thin pseudobulbs can take the light farther away. Pot in firbark, and feed every other watering with high-nitrogen food during bloom period. If you cut the bloom to give it away, do it within one or two joints of the soil. Misting daily is a must, and soil must be moist but not wet. For orchids to bloom, nighttime coolness is the rule; a drop of 10 to 15 degrees is the rule of green thumb.

153

PLANTS UNDER LIGHTS

FIRECRACKER FLOWER

A sunny plant from India to brighten dreary days: *Crossandra infundibuliformis* has upright flower spikes having scarlet-orange flowers; leaves are dark and undulating, similar to the gardenia. It blooms all year under indoor lights or strong filtered sunlight. First try one or two four-inch pots on a tray of pebbles in a breakfast or dining alcove. *Crossandra* is a gilt-edge plant investment with its clear blossoms, its ease in adapting itself to your life. Later look for a plant about 12 inches tall and the same spread for your first dividends.

Water well in summer, moderately in winter, and keep the mister handy because in dry air the leaves may decide to roll up. Too cold water makes brown marks, so always use lukewarm. Feed every two weeks, being sure the soil is damp before applying. It doesn't take to the hot sun, prefers temperatures between 60° and 75°. Prune it flat top, remove senile blossoms weekly to encourage more young. Repot in February in a mixture of two parts peat, one of potting soil and one of coarse sand, in a shallow pot. Childhood ailments are spider mites; misting helps keep them away.

Propagation: cuttings in spring; seeds (bloom should show in nine months).

HEATHER

Also called Christmas heather because it is a winter bloomer, *Erica gracilis* is not true Scotch or Irish heather. It comes from South Africa. But they all resemble one another, having densely set branches and the telltale tubular blossoms.

Erica is a modest-size bush with a vertical habit; it has mini bell flowers, pink to purple, which show early winter and into February. Foliage is fresh green, narrow and scale-like, hugging the branches. In Germany, heather is grown specially for gifting on All Hallow's Day, the first of November. Grown under light, it will now bloom earlier and last longer.

Potting needs: soil on the acid side, or peaty, is its favorite. Give generous watering; if it dries out even once it will drop leaves. Keep heather moist in winter, too, and mist during the warm months. Chlorosis, or yellowing, of the foliage indicates an iron imbalance. Salts left from fertilizing can scorch the roots, so don't feed more than twice a month, and then lightly. When repotting, water well first. Pinch back in spring to keep it bushy—but not after April.

Propagation: cuttings.

HELIOTROPE

What's a nice old-fashioned pot like this doing here? Because it has the good word about living with lights which imitate the sun, that's why. Old English gardens abounded in goodies like *Heliotropium arborescens, Primula,* cinerarias, *Impatiens,* and no one saw the need to take flowering plants out of the garden into the house.

Now that Thomas Edison's gift of lighting has fused with the needs of plants, and so few of us have city garden space, lovely heliotrope moves right in with its lush masses of dark blue-violet, lavender-blue and even white, bringing that nostalgic fragrance, that sunny window radiance, under lights.

Choose a low full shape for artificial lights, perhaps no more than a foot tall. Force bloom January to July by letting the plant rest from September with less water and a cool condition. Shape and encourage by nipping out tops of shoots; repot in spring.

Propagation: cuttings, any time.

MARIGOLD

Marigolds? Indoors? Yes, like heliotrope, these tough little annuals will take to artificial sunlight like the Chinese Evergreen takes to water, and bloom and bloom! *Tagetes patula,* the small French marigold, has fine leaves, rather fern-like, and will give out loads of color all summer if you pick off the old flower heads. You know the colors—pale yellow, orange, maroon, bi-color tangerine. Try to select colors at the nursery so you know they will be simpatico.

There are single and double types which will grow to 15 inches; extra dwarf doubles are about six inches tall. Buy flat-grown plants rather than going the seed route. Ask for the odorless ones in newer varieties.

Tagetes erecta, the African marigold, is too big, too coarse for housebreaking. However, new varieties are interesting dwarfs: Cupid Yellow and Cupid Orange, with two and a half- to three-inch flowers on odorless eight- to ten-inch bushy plants.

Menu calls for ample watering, warmth. Marigolds will also do well in a sunny window.

Propagation: seeds which sprout rapidly in bottom-warmed soil.

155

PLANTS UNDER LIGHTS

MOCK STRAWBERRY

Here's a hardy little ground cover which can be a nuisance in the garden because it runs away with space—but moves indoors to be an amusing docile topiary, thanks to indoor lighting.

Duchesnea indica, also called Indian Mock strawberry, has bright green leaves on long stalks; each has that familiar triad leaf form of the real strawberry, and a small bright red berry which is a phony because it is inedible. The berries grow above the leaves instead of under, and you may have to warn visiting fruit-pickers to lay off. The flexible stems can be wound around a wire frame secured to the pot to make a wreath, or a heart; try your hand at fashioning something out of a wire coat hanger. Pinch back weekly during the growing season.

Mock strawberry needs regular watering and care that the plant never dries out. Feed once a month in spring and summer; add iron chelate if the leaves show signs of yellowing (chlorosis). It may defoliate in winter, but by March young shoots show again.

Propagation: from fruit. Let fruit dry and plant in soil in April.

PRIMROSE

Sure sign of spring, this sassy mass of blooms so familiar to gardeners. And here it is, indoors, along with heliotrope and marigolds and heavens knows how many adopted children of fluorescent lighting. Primrose, *Primula,* is an herbaceous annual, or perennial, depending on which species you try. Three are considered good subjects for light gardens: *Primula malacoides* is an annual, tallest and with largest leaves; it's also called the Fairy primrose. *Primula obconica* is a perennial and also the one which irritates the skin with its hairs; put on your gloves to handle. The *Primula sinensis,* also a perennial, is the small one, rarely over 10 inches, and probably the easiest to get from your garden center.

Repot the latter two when they stop blooming; *P. sinensis* needs to be high in the pot and may even need a little stake. This is to keep the crown free of water. Keep primroses moist, but don't let their feet stand in water. On the other hand, if you forget to water, dunk the whole pot in a lukewarm water bath for an hour. One warning: Keep the roots cool. Plant in clay pots and cover soil around plant with sphagnum moss which you mist to give evaporation. Feed sparingly.

Propagation: seeds, planted on top of the soil, and grown under lights.

APHELANDRA

Q *Is it possible to get more than one bloom on an Aphelandra?*

A *Aphelandra* is one of those mass-produced plants grown for its showy foliage, and usually forced under greenhouse conditions to attract the buyer. Given normal house or apartment conditions, it sags after the showy yellow bloom has breathed its last. If you give it warmth (at least 75°) and humidity of at least 60 percent, it will have a chance to try again. Give it artificial light pick-me-up, and if you have a humidifier, or a wet-pebble tray, it will try even harder. Older plants branch, and cuttings can be made from these for plants better acclimated to your conditions. Under lights, and with misting, they will make it.

BEGONIA

Q *Will you recommend a rule of thumb for growing begonias under lights?*

A Indoor lighting is the green thumb's best friend if you are growing begonias. Give them 14 to 16 hours of light each day. This can be all fluorescent or part natural and part fluorescent. Rex begonias should be placed about 12 to 14 inches from the light source; the Wax can be as close as eight inches. A trip to the outside world is a summer boost and they'll respond to a shaded, out-of-the-wind spot.

Q *The Wax begonias I'm growing under lights get awfully leggy.*

A This happens, even if soil conditions in the house are better than they would get outdoors. By pinching back the new growth constantly you can keep them in line, and expect year-round bloom. Make yourself rooted cuttings and they'll be ready to replace the original plants, or to pot up as contributions for a community fund-raiser.

EPIDENDRUM

Q *How close do I put lights to the Epidendrum?*

A Light experts recommend putting the pot at the edge of the light garden, tilted so that the tip is three to four inches under fluorescent tubes. *Epidendrum* is an easy orchid which goes on and on, blooming.

Q *How do I take a cutting of an Epidendrum?*

A When new stalks start at the bottom of an old one, or there are side growths, called "keikis," they can be separated and potted up in regular firbark orchid mixture. Mist them for higher humidity; feed with orchid-type fertilizer, one high in nitrate.

FIRECRACKER FLOWER

Q *Why do the leaves of my Firecracker flower turn yellow and drop?*

A *Crossandra* wants a constantly moist condition, but too much water and the lower leaves do just what you're unhappy about. If you're growing it under lights, give it a long 16-hour day and lights about five inches away to get extended bloom.

HEATHER

Q *I pruned back my heather and now there's no bloom. Does this mean you can't shape this plant?*

A You can shear *Erica* after the blooming period to stimulate new growth. You need to make the cuts just above an unbloomed side branch—never back into bare wood. Next time cut only wood which has already bloomed.

PLANTS UNDER LIGHTS

CRAPE MYRTLETTE

Q *Someone told me there's a dwarf Crape Myrtle; how can I find one?*

A It should be started from seed (check Seed Sources at end of seed section for the address of Park Seed Company). Seeds germinate rapidly, and you may even see buds before the third month ends. Remove them; the plant is too young to try flowering. Once the branches are five to six inches, it's ready to give out those lovely little bright bunches.

CUPHEA

Q *Can I make cuttings of Cuphea?*

A The Cigar plant or Elfin herb is a small plant, kept in check by constant pinching back. It is the new long thin branches which you cut to propagate. Try starting them in moist vermiculite. Pot up the established cuttings in a moist packaged soil, with a little lime added. Keep them moist, and about 15 inches under the lights.

DWARF POMEGRANATE

Q *Does dwarf pomegranate have fruit?*

A Yes, and the flowers are almost as large on the 15-inch-or-less shrub. It's recommended that you blow into the blossom and this will encourage the fruiting. Warmth and humidity help. (Fruit takes most of the plant's energies so don't try to force more than one at a time.)

HELIOTROPE

Q *The leaves on my heliotrope are dropping off. What would cause this?*

A First, check to see if the *Heliotropium* is pot bound; its roots need plenty of spreading room and must be repotted every spring. Also, it is allergic to overwatering and to too dry conditions.

LOBELIA

Q *Can I start that darling little blue Lobelia from seeds, using artificial light?*

A Plant seeds just below top of a lime-rich soil, and within two months you should have bloom which will last for several months. Plant them indoors in fall for winter color. Put several seedlings in a small clay pot—they like close quarters, cool roots. Place plant top about four inches below lights.

MARIGOLD

Q *Could I plant seeds for marigolds in fall instead of spring to get winter bloom?*

A Growers have always planted for hot summer bloom, but with the advent of fluorescent lights, they can be brought to bloom any time of the year. Look for seeds of the Petite, the dwarf French and the Cupid marigolds; these grow less than 12 inches tall. Germination time to bloom: six weeks. Pinch back to encourage full plants.

PRIMROSE

Q *Is there any special trick to growing primroses?*

A Keep them cool! Grow under lights in a basement where the roots will be cool in summer. Air conditioning will mean *Primula* can be grown upstairs later with the family.

PLANTS TO MATCH AN ENERGY CRISIS

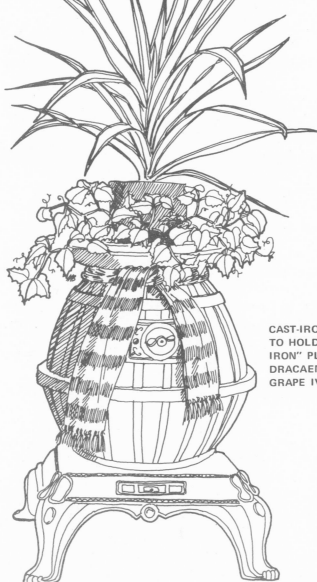

CAST-IRON STOVE
TO HOLD "CAST-
IRON" PLANTS:
DRACAENA &
GRAPE IVY

ENERGY CRISIS PLANTS

Energy crises come in all sizes and shapes, from A (for Arabs) to Z (for zapping weather), circumstances which cut the ground from under one's green dependents. Apartment managers and supers have annoying habits of turning off the heat during the day. Or, a storm knocks out electric lines to the house at the lake—and you're counting on automatic heat to keep the plants alive. Or, a hot tin-roof day brings air conditioner outages.

People suffer. Plants expire. Some plants *can* survive, however, 40° to 55° conditions at night, but need warmth during the day. Flowering types are usually of this nature. Others can stand the 90°-plus days, provided they get constant misting and cooler nights; these are the greenhouse-broken. But in a real energy breakdown, the old "cast-iron" greenies of Victorian days are the only ones to withstand temperature traumas of extreme heat or cold.

Aspidistra, Corn palm *(Dracaena),* most of the figs like Fiddle Leaf and Little Leaf, Snake plant, Fingerleaf and Norfolk Island pine can survive several days of non-cooperative conditions. Hangers-on like Wandering Jew, Spider plant, Grape ivy and Chinese Evergreen have built-in resistance. Asparagus fern can stand a 40° to 50° period without wilting. Mind you, there's a limit to the endurance of these cast-iron greens too; if you surround yourself with plants knowing you are vulnerable, be prepared to retrench.

There are a few rays of hope for plants in an energy crunch. If there is an electric outage, gather all the plants you have adopted into one area, preferably the bath. Run a tub of hot water to take the chill off the room, repeating if necessary. Gas ovens used to warm kitchens will help, but most plants turn up their leaves at the fumes. If there's a gas shutoff, get yourself to a hardware store and stock up on heat lamps (don't forget they have to be used in ceramic sockets).

On a hot day, when the juice disappears and the heat stays, mist your plants several times daily; they transpire more like you perspire so a cooling (not cold) mist will help them through the roughest part. They will probably lose some leaves. Watch particularly for bug problems after a heating up like that.

In an apartment, when you are at the mercy of a stingy thermostat, check temperatures with a thermometer several times in one day to find where the cold spots hide. Put your plants in areas where they'll have better survival chances. Put weather stripping around drafty windows; tape sheets of paper in windows between glass and any plant. Plants grown under incandescent lights get some warmth from the globe.

If you leave a plant in a second home, select one of the cast-iron variety and water well before you leave. Make a tent of clear plastic sheeting over the plant, and this should see it through at least one day of no heat. Beyond that, be prepared to send in replacements.

161

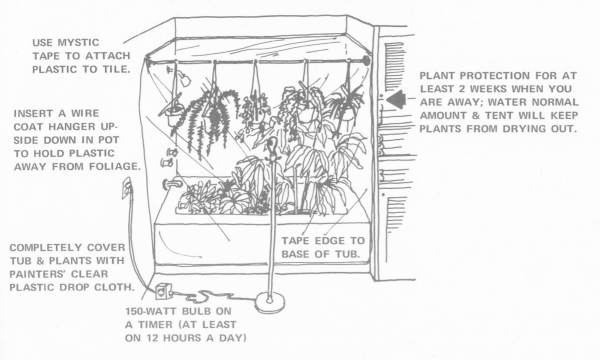

USE MYSTIC TAPE TO ATTACH PLASTIC TO TILE.

INSERT A WIRE COAT HANGER UPSIDE DOWN IN POT TO HOLD PLASTIC AWAY FROM FOLIAGE.

COMPLETELY COVER TUB & PLANTS WITH PAINTERS' CLEAR PLASTIC DROP CLOTH.

PLANT PROTECTION FOR AT LEAST 2 WEEKS WHEN YOU ARE AWAY; WATER NORMAL AMOUNT & TENT WILL KEEP PLANTS FROM DRYING OUT.

TAPE EDGE TO BASE OF TUB.

150-WATT BULB ON A TIMER (AT LEAST ON 12 HOURS A DAY)

ENERGY CRISIS PLANTS

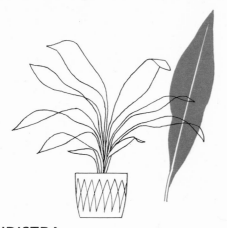

ASPIDISTRA

The original cast-iron, or restaurant, plant has been disinterred, or better, resurrected. The current generation doesn't identify with that past when it was the steadfast and sole greenery in great-grandmama's parlor. They've discovered its postman durability: neither heat nor drought, cold nor drowning stays its appointed daily round. They like having greenery which doesn't sulk from indifference, skimping. They have affinity for its 15- to 30-inch lancet leaves which grow on skinny stems clustered in a small pot.

Aspidistra elatior arrived by way of southern Japan rather than the tropics. It survives down the years, its endurance *is* cast iron, even when given too little light or too much to eat, or gas fumes. *A. elatior variegata* has white striping on its four-inch-wide leaves, but will revert to solid green if the location is too dark. Temperature range of 45° to 85° acceptable, but giving it six warm bright months out of the year will encourage larger, glossier leaves. Misting and bi-weekly fertilizing are bonuses, too.

Propagation: divide fleshy roots in early spring with a sharp knife. Pot several clumps together.

FINGERLEAF PHILODENDRON

Here's yet another *Philodendron, bipinnatifidum,* or Fingerleaf, whose vigor and endurance defy lowered heat and bright illumination. (*P. selloum* is an alternate choice.) There is no climbing stem on the Fingerleaf; the leaves grow from a central self-heading point. Fingerleaf is the largest of this family which survives most crises, and as a furniture substitute will brighten space in a dreary outage, or otherwise. It's hardy but hopefully won't have to deal with too many spells of low temperatures.

Fingerleaf's dark green leaves are up to 20 inches long with equally long stems and have very deep slashes right to the main rib like a giant's fern. They look their best in bright light; brown spots will mark the edges when exposed to direct rays of hot sun, particularly through glass where the temperature can be boosted up to 20°. Central heating, moderate light pose no problems. Soil watered on the good-soaking-to-almost-dry basis seems to work best. As with any *Philodendron,* drainage is important to avoid soggy soil. Light feeding monthly should keep its size within limits. Rare flowering on old plants brings a calla-like bloom with purple outside, white inside. Repot when roots push to surface looking for more room. Use potting soil; don't feed first six months in new container.

Propagation: cuttings.

INDIA LAUREL FIG

Ficus retusa nitida is a small street-tree type which adapts to the move indoors, with the minor annoyance that there may be leaf-fallout for the first couple of weeks. All fig family members are sensitive about moves and the longer acclimated to one place, the more fussy they are about being disturbed. Durable India Laurel is usually sold at a nursery in a container, and leaves have been stripped from the straight trunk, or standard, leaving a thick rounded mass at the top. Leaves are oval shape, waxy and generally healthy.

Put this handsome tree—a pair can solve a dozen decorating problems—in a good light position, out of the sun. It likes warmth, but can stand brief no-heat periods; humidity is a growth factor. Let the soil dry to a depth of several inches before giving a thorough rewatering, and feed once a month. If it seems to be standing still, move to brighter location.

A thrips invasion should be its only threat, and that can be handled without hiring professional help. Use a double or triple application, on a weekly basis, of a liquid systemic poison into the soil, so when the little bugs suck the juices they get zapped. Signs: when leaves get whitish blotches, spotted brown or curl on the edges.

MISTLETOE FIG

This is an offbeat Malaysian fig, not grandiose like the Fiddle Leaf, nor elegant like the *benjamina. Ficus diversifolia* may attain its full growth at two feet, but makes up for its minor size with a handsome form and the appearance of tiny yellow-red, fig-like, non-edible fruit. Your plant source may sell the Mistletoe with the Latin name of *Ficus lutescens;* plant names have a chameleon way of being reclassified.

Mistletoe starts out as a small bushy form; with judicious pruning it can become a larger-than-life bonsai in a couple of years. It develops open twisted branches with stubby round leaves. Each leaf has three minute black spots symmetrically placed on its yellowish underside—they're not scale. Also there will be pinpoint dots on the surface, not caused by bugs.

This fig likes more moisture than others, and should be treated to frequent misting. About feeding, use a high potassium formula. Watch for signs of spider mites; they may appear when the plant is drier. Otherwise, a room deprived of some heat won't set it back, and window light (no sun) will satisfy. Figs are finicky about moving; if the light and heat conditions change, there may be a major leaf drop. Don't worry, more will come.

163

ENERGY CRISIS PLANTS

SNAKE PLANT

Sansevieria trifasciata sticks its tongue out at dark corners and parental neglect. If ever a plant disconnected itself from trouble, this is it. Energy crises are put down with indifference. The tough vertical-growing leaves are twisty, with light horizontal markings. *Sansevieria laurenti,* from the Congo, has three- to four-foot sword leaves, mottled and edged in pale yellow. *S. parva* is small, trails, and will do in a basket. Flowers on the Snake appear when the plant is pot bound, on leafless stalks. They're scented and green-yellow, and not very amusing.

Repotting is necessary only should cracks appear in the clay pot indicating too many roots for the space. Use a general purpose mixture, with feeding about three times a year—and *don't* overwater.

Give the Snake plant (also called Bow String Hemp, or Mother-in-Law's Tongue) shade and winter watering, just enough to keep leaves from shriveling; give it sun and normal summer watering, and you've been an adequate parent.

Propagation: cut a leaf in three-inch sections, plant cut lower edge in sand; young plant will have plain green unmottled leaves.

STRIPED DRACAENA

This is our old friend, the Corn palm, in another costume: Stiff but yielding leaves, up to 24 inches long and two inches wide, have rows of white and gray stripes lengthwise. Leaves grow around and up a cane-like stem. The main difference between the Corn palm and *Dracaena deremensis warnecki* is the slimness and elegance and coloration of the latter. Both do well in bright light, existing room temperatures, with casual watering and low humidity. Which is not to say that they wouldn't rush headlong with proper love and tender care.

Dracaena d. warnecki makes an impressive background for a collection of smaller plants on pedestals, or flower collections. *Dracaena marginata* has clusters of 12- to 15-inch red-edge leaves, perhaps half an inch wide, which burst in all directions from a center stem, like the yucca. The Dragon tree, *D. massangeana,* puts its energy in tufts of leaves at the tips of gyrating cane-like trunks.

The Striped *Dracaena* is a good narrow-corner plant and it could threaten the ceiling one day. That's the time to remove two or three feet from the stem, and propagate a new striper by rooting the tip in water. Remove all leaves from the bottom third of the cutting. Repot the rooted plant in packaged soil and hold out feeding for the first six months.

ASPIDISTRA

Q *My Aspidistra looks dull; is there anything I can give it to brighten up the leaves?*

A A sponging with water will keep the dust off. An addition of a teaspoon of Volck to a quart of tepid water, used for sponging, will give the leaves a longer-time shine. *Aspidistra* leaves respond to more light and will look sharper for it.

FIDDLE LEAF FIG

Q *I've had a Fiddle Leaf fig for eight years and now there are little round knobs growing.*

A Although the *Ficus lyrata* or *F. pandurata* is not supposed to fruit, an old one will bear hard fig-like ones. They're not edible, just conversation gambits.

Q *Why would the leaves of my Fiddle Leaf drop?*

A The soil around the roots has probably dried out recently. *Ficus* needs thorough watering and then to be left until almost dry. Often the soil top may seem dry but if you bury your index finger a couple of inches, the soil will tell you if it's time to water again.

IVY

Q *What can I do to make an ivy plant more interesting than just a hanging pot?*

A Any of the *Hedera* are easy to train on wire forms; take your pot down from the ceiling and make yourself a growing sculpture. Buy a wire frame from a garden center; secure it in the pot and make a topiary. Make a bamboo or lath trellis and lash the ivy to it. Bend a wire coat hanger into a simple diamond shape. By weaving the ivy branches and pinching back to a pleasant shape, you can lead the plant to a brand new look.

Q *My ivy looks straggly and the leaves are far apart.*

A Ivy needs a cool room and good light to live happily, and it should have a moist but never soggy soil. Leaves are far apart because light level is too low. Move the ivy; check the drainage.

Q *I keep my ivy cool but there are some kind of little black things on the plant. I sprayed but they're still there.*

A Black aphids, or plant lice, are the most discouraging problem with ivies. Take the plant outside and turn the hose spray on it to wash them off; this is an important step before spraying. After the hosing, spray a mild solution of Malathion and when it dries, rinse with the hose again. The only defense for dealing with aphids is to examine leaves each time you water, and pinch off any which show signs of the nasties. If there's a particularly solid colony, cut off the branch and destroy it. Cutting back is good for renewed growth.

KANGAROO TREEBINE

Q *Is it possible for Kangaroo vine to get mealy bug? I keep mine cool, I mist it—but there are those funny bits of cotton on the stems.*

A It certainly is possible. The mealy bug is a scale insect, having a soft white waxy look instead of the hard brown caps on the other form. They both suck the juices from plant tissues causing plants to wilt, defoliate. If the infestation is minor, use a cotton swab dipped in rubbing alcohol on each white bump. Otherwise, take the plant outside and spray with a systemic solution, once a week for three weeks.

ENERGY CRISIS PLANTS

SNAKE PLANT

Q *I thought the Snake plant was cast-iron, but mine looks like an old flatiron.*

A Overwatering or poor drainage are the only things which might do in your *Sansevieria*. The remedy is to dunk the pot in a bucket of lukewarm water to wet it completely through; let the plant go through a drying cycle and repeat. Check the drainage hole to be sure it's not closed off by soil or roots.

UMBRELLA TREE

Q *My big Umbrella tree has dropped all its leaves at the bottom of the stems and imitates a palm tree. Is there any way to force new growth at the bottom?*

A Older *Schefflera* plants make offsets at the base if the living is easy: bright light, morning or late afternoon sun, extra misting and a thorough soaking each time you water. Heat and moisture, night temperature readings above 65° are its hang-ups. Feed high-phosphate diet every six months. If nothing happens after following these suggestions, prepare for surgery: air layer the trunks, cut off the tops when the roots form and dispose of the old plant.

There's another way to look at the schefflera. Accept the "palm" look, and fill the foreground with a collection of potted plants like caladium, coleus, croton, or buy two small schefflera and set the pots at the base of the old-timer.

WANDERING JEW

Q *Is there any way I can stop the leaves of my Wandering Jew from falling?*

A One reason for this is that the plant can't support a big family, and it is asking you to pinch it back. People hesitate removing new growth, but it's better than letting the plant get leggy and scrawny and drop leaves. Taking off the lower leaves lets the *Tradescantia* or *Zebrina* make more new ones. Another reason for leaf-fall is overwatering; leaves will go limp and turn yellow. If the plant has been neglected and dried out, leaves will curl and drop.

Q *I bought a purple Wandering Jew but now the leaves look pale.*

A The more light it gets, the deeper the purple.

Q *When I selected the Tahitian Bridal Veil I was told its botanical name was Gibasis. A friend says it is a Wandering Jew. Which is right?*

A *Gibasis* is one of the family of spiderworts, of which Wandering Jew is the collective name. Bridal Veil is sold also as *Tripogandra multiflora* or *Tradescantia multiflora*. It can be treated like any of the family: modest light, moisture and an indifference about temperature.

ALOE

**PLANTS YOUR
CAT WON'T
NIBBLE:
SUCCULENTS
AND CACTI**

VERY OLD
PENCIL
CACTUS

BALL
CACTUS

OPUNTIA

OLD MAN
CACTUS

LITHOPS

SECTIONS OF
LOG OR OLD
TELEPHONE
POLE

AGAVE

I'm only teasing. There are other ways to tempt your wayward feline or the family puppy away from your green pets. (If your *gato* is green-hungry, raise a little bluegrass lawn in an aluminum Sara Lee cake pan full of peat moss and potting soil. Seed and water it, and add the light of a fluorescent. It should satisfy his urge for chloro-fill.)

It's just that taste can have nine lives, too. Some lifestyles don't allow palms or Passion vines to dominate. There are free spirits growing *Pachypodium,* a rare big desert creature covered with thorns and an umbrella of thin green leaves, in a La Jolla bank; decorators search for collections of Peruvian and Mexican Old Man cacti for a veep's suite in a Tulsa TV station. And a second grade class in Tacoma proudly fills every windowsill with yoghurt cups planted with fat species of *Mammillaria.* Individual taste in assembling, in decorating is the word for Plant Lib. Being a plant parent, you can understand this. Right? Can a Creeping Charlie type find happiness with a Rattail cactus? Yes.

Does being a father to a begonia collection mean you are retired, settled and conservative? No way. Stockbrokers, halfbacks and paperhangers have discovered how to deal with tensions by filling basements and closets with indoor lighting and scores of rhizomatous and Rex begonias blooming their heads off. Meanwhile, 10-year-old Girl Scouts in the next block focus on succulents and cacti lovingly assembled in an old bookcase, for more than just a badge—for fun. Macho junior executives haunt eclectic plant shops for rare *Euphorbia* and Beavertails and chubby Bunny Ears.

Consider the neat forms cacti and succulents take: round and contorted, pencil-slim or droll and fat. They range in size from the pea-shape *Lithops* to giant *Saguaro* which may weigh 20 tons (too big to bring back alive in your VW). They put forth extravagant flowerings, among the biggest in the plant world. They got those forms the hard way. Fifty million years ago in its adolescence the earth was tropic jungle. As a few million more years zinged by, changes came when the surface split with volcanic facelifts; there were new areas left with drought, erosion. Plant life in these places had to learn to economize to survive. Leaves covered themselves with hair, resin or rolled up into needles. Branches became thin, hard; outer layers got tough, sap turned sticky and thick. Plants learned to grow in the shade of rocks, to store every drop of precious moisture.

When you compare these desert plants to a normal blade of grass which transpires its weight in water daily or an apple tree which gives off a couple thousand gallons in the normal growing period, you can see why a succulent hoards the water from a single shower for its yearly quota. Mother Nature is one smart parent. For all their sufferings she made them the most fascinating of her plants, throwing in a little irony and laughter for flavor.

P.S. If your cat *does* persist in being nosy, the thorn can be tweezed out. For humanoids, a dripping of hot wax on the transferred barb will bring it out when the wax has solidified and is pulled away from the skin. Reminder: Avoid mixing with the *Euphorbia,* particularly the Crown of Thorns—its milk is poisonous.

In addition to the plants described on the following pages, other plants your cat won't nibble are: *Aeonium,* Burro Tail, Candle plant, Christmas cactus, *Echeveria, Haworthia,* Mistletoe cactus, Prickly Pear, *Kalanchoe.*

CACTUS IN AN OPEN TERRARIUM

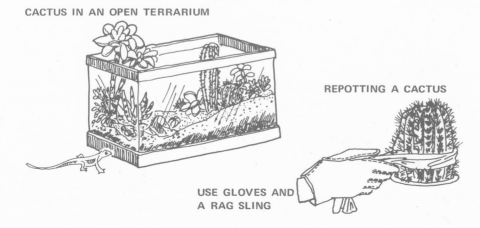

REPOTTING A CACTUS

USE GLOVES AND A RAG SLING

SUCCULENTS AND CACTI

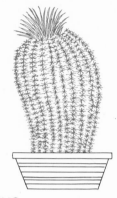

BALL CACTUS

Also identified as Barrel cactus and (by some early chauvinistic relative) as Mother-in-Law Chair. *Echino-cactus* is a large globe with strongly marked ribs, it is filled with a juicy pulp and armored with spines. Storytellers would have you believe that a thirst-mad desert traveler can get water here. It would take a powerful man to get past the spines, to open the ball, and to mash the pulp—which tastes vile anyway! However, Mexicans make an insipid candy for tourists from it, proving there's no accounting for thirst. They make fishhooks from the barbed yellow spines.

This cactus is pure sculpture. A big one, perhaps a foot in diameter, in a pot worthy of its form, is awesome. Obviously it won't do for child-filled households with its Iron Maiden complex. It *is* for a balcony, a multi-level studio, a hair-styling salon, on a pedestal as kingpin for lesser cacti.

Repot in spring with great caution for your hands. Keep old plants dry during winter; give young ones stingy monthly applications—but *don't* feed. After the long rest, steep pot in lukewarm water for a few hours, let drip-dry.

Propagation: easy with seeds, but start young—this is a slow ball game.

CALICO HEARTS, ETC.

Calico Hearts, Sea Shells, Pretty Pebbles, Plover's Eggs—sound like plant names? You peeked! They're all relatives of the species *Adromischus* and just happen to be about the easiest succulents to grow. They're friendly little shapes, ingeniously colored, and requiring about four hours of sunlight a day, and water only when they're dry, from spring to fall. Keep them almost dry in winter, in a cool room.

Calico Hearts, *Adromischus maculatus,* has thick stemless one- and two-inch leaves which lie flat in an overcrowded pot, each little overlapping heart wearing red-brown marks on a mossy green lid. Sea Shells, *A. cristatus,* have a pie shape with undulating edge; Pretty Pebbles, *A. clavifolius,* have blunt ends and are muted green with red markings; Plover's Eggs are mimics with their egg-shape bluish leaves and red-purple spots.

These plants show off in shallow three- and four-inch clay or white ceramic saucers. If repotting, plan to do it in April, using a well-mixed, half-and-half of soil and sharp sand with a dollop of limestone and bonemeal. Don't feed the newly potted succulent for at least a year. Feed once a year thereafter.

Propagation: leaf cuttings.

COB CACTUS

The Cob cactus, or *Lobivia,* has a different set of demands. It comes down out of the high Andes, asking for bone-dry chill winter, 40° to 45°. This cold storage is to insure the brilliant color and silky flowering. *Lobivia* is shaped like a cob of corn growing vertically out of the soil. But in a mobilization of a dozen in one 12-inch flat clay bowl it becomes one of the handsomest families of small cacti, and an asset to any executive credenza or doctor's atrium. Because its needs are simple, being its parent is easy.

The flowers appear on the short cobs, perhaps only four to six inches tall, which are lined with spines. They open four inches wide to reveal orange, scarlet and deep yellow. That's why a small forest in a large flat bowl, basking in the sun, is a magic turn-on for collectors. Warmth is also necessary until the winter rest starts. Don't attempt this cactus unless you can meet its winter needs.

Propagation: from young cobs which appear on the sides of the main trunk.

DUDLEYA

Here is a wildly colorful winter-show succulent for your first collection, when all the rest of the cacti are sleeping. The *Dudleya* easiest to locate is *Dudleya brittonii.* It hails from sunny Baja California and Mexico. Long ago *Dudleya* bought its life insurance against herbiverous desert animals by developing a repulsive quinine-flavor interior. Luckily for collectors, the odor stays inside, and only the desert rats are double-crossed.

The rosette form of the *D. brittonii* is a foot wide, the leaves cupped and tapering. The flowering occurs on tall tapers which stretch above the rosette. *Dudleya pulverulenta,* Chalk Lettuce, grows larger in an 18-inch rosette, and is silver gray and mealy. Both species have leaves which are fleshy and covered with a heavy dusting of chalky powder (you can wipe it off if it shows bruise marks).

Propagation: seeds, or leaves which can be removed by gently twisting, and are planted two together, bases touching, in sand. Don't water until roots form and only a little then; repot in sandy loam, keeping heat above 60°.

SUCCULENTS AND CACTI

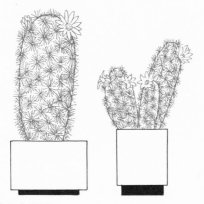

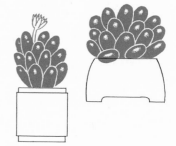

MAMMILLARIA

There are over 240 collectible members of this family, and only the general characteristics can be abstracted in this limited space. *Mammillaria* are most familiar in the shape of a globe, but others, like *M. elongata* are multi-chimney pots with many-color spines and wool in the axils.

To distinguish from the Ball cactus, these have lines of bumps with stars of spines in each bump and a dense covering of white hairs. The flower-producing spots lie in between. *M. elongata* has a bright yellow crown of small blossoms. Snowball Pincushion, *M. candida,* begins as a single globe, two to three inches tall, which eventually increases to several smaller ones with clustered wooly blankets and angelic tiny white flowers on the tips.

Some have watery sap and can take more watering in the warm months; milky sap ones need less. They grow slowly to at least a foot tall, whether at sea level or 8,000 feet in rare air. Most important, put the *Mammillaria* in the sun for at least four hours a day, temperature 60° to 85°. In winter keep cool and water only to keep from withering.

Propagation: take small new plants from side of main cactus.

MOONSTONES

Pachyphytum are succulents, amusing fat leaves attached to thick stems. The leaf is almost egg-shaped, and is flushed with lavender and pink. Being overweighted, the heavy stems tend to flop over the pot rim as they get older while the younger ones fill to a height of about six inches. These leaves tend to get even more opalescent coloration if given a good share of the day's sun. Let the little *Pachyphytum* go almost dry between waterings in spring, summer and fall; in winter add just enough to keep them from losing that charming weight in water.

Succulents, taken as a group, dislike low light and will expire—a pitiful sight. I planted a huge Chinese ceramic fish with *Pachyphytum oviferum* and *Echeveria* as a decorating experiment, but within four weeks of light-starving on the dining table, they began to look like basket cases. Try them under fluorescents on a 16-hour day schedule for sun substitution. Moonstones can be fed once a year in spring with liquid or cacti plant food, but only half strength although everyone loves a fat *Pachyphytum.*

Propagation: leaf cuttings.

OLD MAN CACTUS

Every collector tries *Cephalocereus* at some point. *C. senlis,* the Mexican Old Man cactus, is usually available in pots, from eight inches to a foot tall. It takes veneration, lots of years, to get its full stature, the heavy white beard and the one- and two-inch needles which make it formidable.

C. chrysacanthus, the Golden Old Man, has 10 to 12 bluish ribs, and short yellow hair over shorter spines. Other collectors' prizes include Peruvian O.M., *Espostoa lanata,* and O.M. of the Andes, *Oreocereus celsianus.* Picture a dozen of these venerable characters sitting out their lives on a tall Chinese prayer table, soaking up the sun in the resigned ways of old men, and you can understand the fierce devotion of a *Cephalocereus* fancier.

A layer of sand around the cactus neck helps the roots resist rot when accidentally overwatered. Keep quite dry and not too close to window glass to overheat. P.S. If the hair gets dusty, wash it with a tepid solution of real soapsuds, rinse and dry with your hair blower.

Propagation: stem cuttings.

OX-TONGUE GASTERIA

Gasteria sticks out its tongues to typical succulent forms, and makes a flat fan of disarmingly smooth leaves. The leaves are marbled with tiny pale tubercles, or bumps, where spines may once have emerged, but the tongue shape of the leaves is their important characteristic. These tongues grow first one direction, then directly opposite the next, and as the new ones come they grow vertically, forcing old ones to horizontal status. Put several on a coffee table as back-up to a tribe of tiny succulents. All grouped in a blue laquered tray (from your local discount import house) create a very personal expression.

Gasteria verrucrosa is easiest to find, but don't ignore it if you're collecting. Pink and purple flowers hang in soft curves at the end of stems; they have an obvious bulb at the base. Start with one six inches tall in a small pot. They like cramped quarters and tolerate neglect, but are less tongue-tied in rich well-drained soil and good light. Keep out of direct sun—save that space for the cacti. Temperature range from 50° to 72°; water when moderately dry and feed once a year with dilute fish emulsion.

Propagation: offsets.

173

SUCCULENTS AND CACTI

PEBBLE PLANTS

Pebble plants impersonate pebbles. Here is the ultimate in survival: Chubby little plant bodies sprinkle themselves among rounded stones, hoping that an herb-hungry creature will run right past. *Lithops* are plants as small as three-eighths of an inch up to three inches across, cylindrical leprechaun stools (no stem), and about equal measurements wide. They grow with two "leaves" which are joined facing one another and separated only by a cleft in the center, like a screw head. The top is a ringer for river-washed pebbles—except that out of the cleft come large anemone-like flowers, and a whole pot planted with *Lithops* becomes an oriental carpet of color in summer.

Full sun is in order and the hotter the better. Water with a stingy hand, and in winter cut back to zero. Grow a collection in tiny separate pots, then sink several into a large gravel-filled tray; this prevents root scorch in the individual pot. After the flowering and seed period, Pebble plants are dormant. They wither and whiten. Then, one day, they break open to reveal a brand new pair of leaves.

Propagation: by division. Use small gravel, sandy loam and a pinch of peat. Seeds, also.

RATTAIL CACTUS

A thin whip of a "leaf" has a mouthful of a name: *Aporocactus flagelliformis*—and a more non-cactus look you may not find. It looks great in a hanging pot, forming a fountain of green with a great fireworks show of rich red and pink bloom in spring. The *Aporocactus* has short golden spines on its half-inch thick whips, or tails. Collectors who like to fool Mother Nature take their fun in grafting the tails on top of an unsuspecting plain columnar cactus of some height—giving the look of an explosion.

Cacti have a unique affinity for one another, and this grafting is not too complicated. A sterile knife dipped in alcohol is used to cut off the top of the new parent with one clean stroke; bevel the edges, leaving a little platform. The Rattail is removed from its pot, roots sliced off and rim beveled upward, and the two cut ends pressed together. Plan this job so you put them together as cleanly and quickly as possible. Put a weight on top for a week to hold the graft. Keep temporarily shaded.

Rattail requires rich soil, four hours sun daily, and 65° to 85° spring through fall. Keep moderately dry between waterings.

Propagation: stem cuttings.

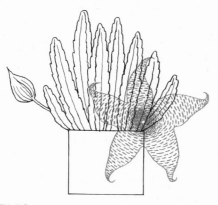

STAPELIA

Stapelia, which ranges in size from three inches to three feet, is an out-and-out succulent—and also a member of the milkweed family, showing clearly again how displaced plant families change their spots. *Stapelia* resembles cacti with its groups of thick four-sided stems. They carry the tubercle marks where primitive leaves have long since disappeared. The blossom is a Joseph's-coat-of-all-colors, mainly yellow with dots of deep red.

Stapelia is also called Starfish flower and unhappily for some, Carrion flower. The latter comes from the offbeat "fragrance" which is a kind of plant B.O. unabated by Right Guard. When the five-point star flower appears—up to 18 inches across in some species—its scent attracts blow flies. Pollen is so locked into the bloom that it can only be transferred by the flies. Their feet get caught in the sticky pollen. When they free themselves they go right on to the next flower, and the basic contact is made.

Pot in a good cactus soil, with good drainage. Give moderate water March through summer, and from September keep it almost dry. Likes dry air, too.

Propagation: cuttings of shoots.

TREE AGAVE

Admittedly, the tree can get too big for its share of space, but in its adolescence the soft gray rosette is captivating. And because it is unarmed it will fit almost any family room. *Agave attenuata* is just one of 300 species, poses no cultural problems, has good manners and is a genuine conversation piece. Give it lots of sun and warmth, a space by itself, and you have the gentle relative of that great spiny, *Agave americana,* the Century plant.

Rigid fleshy leaves grow in a rosette which lifts upward toward the sun like a symmetrical vase. Only older plants flower, but then they die, so enjoy the adolescent and ignore the bloom. Tree *Agave* will be equally at home in a pad filled with pillows, on a stair landing of the Queen Mary or on a retirement home balcony. Don't let it scare you—there are people who make great pets of wolves, and there are those individual enough to adopt *Agave.*

Furnish water in larger amounts in summer in contrast to other cacti, but follow the rule for a dry winter. Give a dilute feeding every other week, May through August.

Propagation: by offsets at the base; set in a half sand, half soil mixture, and do *not* feed the first year.

175

SUCCULENTS AND CACTI

BALL CACTUS

Q *Someone gave me a live Ball cactus from the desert. How do I keep it alive?*

A First find a clay pot just one inch wider than the diameter of the plant, put shards in the bottom and add a handful of charcoal. Firm the soil mixture around the roots and bring it level to where the cactus was in its former bed. Use tough leather gloves or wrap the *Echinocactus* with folds of soft cloth so you don't ruin hands playing this ball game.

BURRO TAIL

Q *I inherited a Burro Tail in a basket. How often should I feed it?*

A Don't, at least not like other plants. I find that adding a teaspoon of bonemeal to the new soil when repotting *Sedum* in a six-inch pot gives adequate push for a whole year—and succulents and cacti don't like to be pushed.

CHRISTMAS CACTUS

Q *My Christmas cactus never blooms. What am I doing wrong?*

A For one thing, this cactus doesn't like to be moved around. For another, it hates drafts, and despises being near a heater or radiator. Also, it must have a long-night rest period (almost all succulents need this to have blooms). Starting in October (the one time you can move it easily, except outdoors in summer) put the plant in a cool, dim place. By November, check for signs of growth, water a couple of times a week and bring the cactus back to a light zone. Add a little plant food to the water and it should show signs of bloom. Yellowing of foliage comes from too much heat, water.

ECHEVERIA

Q *My house has a water softener. Will this affect my Echeveria when I water?*

A Sorry, most water softener formulas contain sodium, which is salt—natural enemy of all house plants. Save rainwater, buy bottled water because succulents don't use much. Remember to never let any water stand in the saucer under a succulent.

ORCHID CACTUS

Q *The buds drop off my Orchid cactus before they open. Am I giving it too much moisture?*

A Surprisingly, I would think the plant can stand more humidity: spare the watering and spray with a mister twice a day. Avoid big changes in temperature. *Epiphyllum* can't stand hot noonday sun, so give it shade; try an east window.

POINSETTIA

Q *My poinsettia has stopped blooming ... now what should I do?*

A As soon as the bright red "bracts" fall, set the *Euphorbia* outside; when weather warms, sink the pot in the garden soil if you have a garden. Otherwise, keep in a shaded place and water only enough to keep it from withering. Prune back to six-inch stalks in early May. Continue watering with a mild feeding every three weeks. Bring indoors in September. To bloom again they must have short-day light for one month, not more than 10 hours. That means room light, street light or TV can interrupt the flowering cycle. P.S. Poinsettia *is* a succulent.

CACTUS POTTING

Q *How do I water a newly potted cactus?*

A When potting, particularly if the roots have been cut or bruised, add *no* water and keep plant and soil dry for a few days, then water sparingly during the first month. This allows roots to heal, or callus; they tend to rot if dampened immediately. P.S. Don't feed the first year after repotting.

INSECTS

Q *A friend says cacti never have bugs. Is this true?*

A A plant is a plant, whether it has green leaves or is a cactus with yellow spines; mealy bugs and scale don't know the difference. Cacti are also susceptible to crown rot and root rot disease—and to overwatering. Mealy is a soft-cover kind of scale, both being sap suckers. A cotton swab dipped in rubbing alcohol gets a minor infestation; if it's bad, spray weekly for three weeks with a systemic solution.

SOIL

Q *Do succulents take a special kind of soil?*

A They're not fussy, but do thrive on a richer mix than you might expect. Try one part sharp sand, one part packaged cactus soil (if you use garden loam add one part leaf mold, too), and one-half part crushed charcoal. To the mixture, for each gallon, add a tablespoon of limestone and one of bonemeal. They do not thrive in plain old sand, believe me.

SUCCULENT ROOTS

Q *Do succulents have roots like other plants?*

A Yes. However, when rooting a cutting, give the cut end a period of rest before putting it in soil. Be sure everything is as clean as possible in this action to avoid transferring any pests or spores. Big cuttings will need support of rocks or bricks around the trunk, or temporary staking, until they root. A rootless plant will shift when moved, but it develops resistance as the roots grow.

SUMMERING OUTDOORS

Q *Can I put my succulent collection outdoors in the summer?*

A Yes. Group your cacti and succulents on a patio or deck with good light but protected from the hot noonday sun. If you have a garden, sink the pots to the rims in soil; bring them back inside before the frosts. Give a cool rest from November to March.

TERRARIUMS

Q *If succulents like dry conditions, why plant them in terrariums?*

A A terrarium can be a dry environment, too. It's simply a matter of leaving the top off, and starting out with minimal moisture. Actually the glass room offers an ideal way to display a collection of small plants like the *Lithops* and Calico Hearts: Spread an inch of coarse gravel, a layer of gardeners' charcoal and the suggested soil mix—*not* level on top but with mounds and swales to arrange a natural scene. Finish off the planting with rocks, stones, coarse sand and place in a bright window.

AND PLANTS FOR GRANDPARENTHOOD

CERAMIC AVOCADO STARTER

Young children in our mobile society get cheated out of much direct communication with their grandparents. Often holidays and vacations are the only get-together times—times usually filled with adult action. This year, try something different: a grandparent-grandchild indoor gardening project. Here are some suggestions. Remember, don't do it for them, Grandparent: Lead them to it, then stand back to watch, to answer questions, to applaud.

WEIGHT TO BEND **TIE**

A NEW TWIST FOR AVOCADOS

AVOCADO: Pick as ripe an avocado as you can find, remove seed and rinse; let it sit overnight, cut a thin sliver off both ends with a razor blade, add three toothpicks poked around seed's equator and set round bottom in water up to toothpicks, to root.

BEET & CARROT TOP PARK: One-inch slices of tops with trimmed greens, set in a tray of water and kept moist, will grow tall new tops in no time.

GRAPEFRUIT SEEDS, removed and dried for two days, then soaked overnight, will grow fast in loose soil; cover with plastic wrap until leaves show.

COCONUT IN A POTTERY CHICKEN

AVOCADO FOREST: GROW 8 OR 10 TOGETHER!

GRAPEFRUIT & LIME BONSAI IN MILK CARTON

COCONUT: Select a large ripe one; leave the husk on as this is the new plant's only nourishment source. Place it in a pan, on a bed of sand, depression end up about 10 degrees higher than the tip; water daily in the depression at the fat end and the crack where sprout starts. Add warmth, lots of sun and faithful spraying.

GINGER ROOT planted in an empty half coconut shell: Make two drainage holes with an ice pick, fill shell with half sand, half vermiculite and plant a ginger section with sprouted points above soil. Add warmth, daily moisture lightly, light.

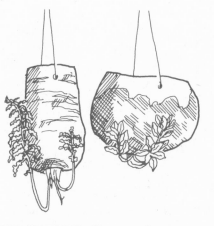

POTATO in a glass flask or hyacinth jar: Try a yam or sweet potato with budding "eyes," at least half submerged in water and in bright light. Roots seek water, leaves appear at top in no time.

CARROT FERN: Choose a fat carrot or rutabaga, cut off one-third of tip; scoop out inside of top with potato peeler, push a wire through open end and hang upside down; keep hole filled with water.

179

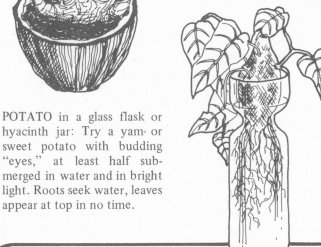

BRIGHT COLOR WATERPROOF COVER

CLAMP-ON PLANT LIGHT IN CERAMIC SOCKET

TOMMIE'S HOUSE

COVERED COFFEE CANS

1 x 4 BOARDS

TIE

PLASTIC DROP CLOTH CUT TO FIT

MAKE A GRANDCHILD A CARD TABLE GREENHOUSE FOR CHRISTMAS

Early success with raising green automatically colors a whole lifetime's interest. This portable unit insures quick, sure success. Seeds and seedlings, flowers will pop out under the plant light. Kids learn about over- and underwatering, how to watch for bugs, how to recognize plant strengths, weaknesses; also to develop interest in outdoor growing.

And the card table is always easily retrievable.

Call the Doctor

Plant parenthood has its share of two-aspirin headaches. There will be times when a plant isn't looking the way you expect it should. Leaves turn brown on the edges (overwatering?), or buds fall off before they have time to open (over-fertilizing? temperature too high at night?). You press the panic button.

There are two possible diagnoses: wrong care or feeding, and invasion of insects. Looking at the sick plant and its soil can give a plant doctor signals or clues. However, if you are new at saving green lives, start learning those signals immediately: Look closely at the leaves and stems. If you don't see telltale marks of insects like uneven curling of leaves (too much light causes edges to turn down uniformly), blotches, trails, webs, scale or white fuzz, then there must be some care and feeding formulas which have gone sour.

A third problem, foreign agents in the soil, like nematodes, earthworms, fungus spores and molds, is harder to identify, even by experts. Therefore, always pot plants in sterilized soil and pots; you automatically eliminate these fiends.

"WHERE DID WE GO WRONG?"

TOO MUCH LIGHT: Many plants can't stand direct sunlight in summer but like winter sun; some naturally grow in shade.

NOT ENOUGH LIGHT: Plants depend on light to make food; this process is called photosynthesis. Plants take advantage of light, can store up against gray days, and form sturdier seeds.

TEMPERATURE TOO HIGH: Nighttime heat saps vigor and growth; interferes with normal blossoming.

TEMPERATURE TOO LOW: Slows down plant's ability to make food; if the plant has to live in cooler than normal conditions several days, cut back on food and water.

OVERWATERING AND POOR DRAINAGE: Drowns the tiny rootlets which are dependent on oxygen to grow; nutrients are not absorbed and plant slowly dies.

LACK OF WATER: Even cacti and succulents need water.

COMPACTED SOIL: Roots can't grow and drainage is impaired.

DRAFTS: A cross draft robs water from foliage and bloom; keep a plant out of any spot where air moves between an often opened door and an open window. A cold draft can be murder.

LENGTH OF DAY: Some plants, like poinsettia and Christmas cactus, depend on long nights of absolute darkness before they will blossom; others, like African violet, need long-light days.

AIR POLLUTION: Faulty gas appliances leaking can make a plant turn up its toes; coal gas from a furnace and auto pollution take a toll.

181

CALL THE DOCTOR

FOLIAGE SIGNALS

Q *Are tips or margins brown?*

A Overwatering; letting the plant dry out completely; fertilizer salt overdose from too much feeding; air pollution.

Q *Do the edges bend down and curl?*

A Too close to artificial light, or too much light; continued exposure to low temperature; air pollution.

Q *Are leaves turning yellow?*

A Lack of iron; too much or too little light; too high temperature at night; compacted soil which means poor drainage.

Q *Old leaves drop off?*

A Too little light; too high temperature at night; overwatering; too much fertilizer; drafts.

Q *All the leaves drop off?*

A Overwatering or letting plant dry out; pollution. No hope for this one.

Q *Brown spots on the leaves?*

A Exposure to hot sun; underwatering; too cool.

Q *Has the plant wilted?*

A Exposure to hot sun, too much light; too warm at night; lack of water; compacted soil, poor drainage; drafts; root shock from repotting.

GROWTH PROBLEMS

Q *Branches are weak, thin or soft?*

A Inadequate light; temperature too high, day or night; overwatering; lack of fertilizer; compacted soil, poor drainage.

Q *New leaves stay small?*

A Inadequate light; temperature too high; overwatering or poor drainage; air pollution.

Q *No new leaves?*

A Temperature too low; lack of water; too much fertilizer and roots can't use it.

UNSATISFACTORY BLOSSOMING

Q *Buds fail to develop, drop off?*

A Lack of light; temperature too high or low for that particular plant; too little or too much water; too much fertilizer and new leaves force buds to drop; poor drainage; length of day: some need more, some less; air pollution.

Q *Is the color less intense?*

A Insufficient light; overwatering, poor drainage; lack of high-phosphorus fertilizer.

Q *Do blooms fade away too fast?*

A Temperature too high at night; lack of water; drafts; air pollution.

Q *Are the flowers small or scarce?*

A Insufficient light; lack of fertilizer; poor drainage.

Q *No blooms at all?*

A Insufficient light; temperature too high at night (orchids have to have a 15-degree cooler night than day to bloom); length of daylight, called photoperiodism: some need more, some less.

INSECTS AND OTHER PREDATORS

No plant is immune to sneaky attacks from aphids, mealy bug, root rot. The plant you adopt may have picked up something at the nursery; tiny sugar ants and flies ferry insects from one plant to another. The only solution is vigilance. Watch for those telltale signals which match the sketch on the next page. Isolate an enemy-bugged pot immediately and start treatment; if you let the invasion get ahead of you, you lose.

Direct treatment, like washing or dunking leaves in soapy water, or applying alcohol to the critters, is the first order of action. Use Ivory or Fels Naptha to make the suds; Basic H, a household cleaner sold in health food stores, makes a sure solution against red spider mites, aphids. Systemic treatment, either sprayed on leaves or scraped into the soil as the manufacturer directs, will be absorbed in the plant's system and bring victory over sucking insects. (Systemic substances are poison; avoid where children or pets can touch. Spray systemic or plant sprays outdoors, away from people things.)

Fungus spores sneak in when conditions are over-moist and air movement is nil. Soft brown spots on the stems, black spots inside discolorations on leaves: trim or discard any infected places. Treat stem and cuts with sulphur dust and increase ventilation.

Root rot is a fungus spore condition too—and very contagious by direct contact. Sterilizing pots before using removes this threat. Let the soil dry out between waterings at any sign of this problem; use a solution of a tablespoon of household bleach to each gallon of water to moisten soil again instead of just water. Malathion, according to directions, will affect root rot; *Crassula* are the exception—they are highly allergic to Malathion.

CALL THE DOCTOR: INSECTS

IF A HOUSE PLANT HAS BEEN BUGGED:

1. Isolate the sick plant immediately.
2. If it's a large plant, wash each leaf with a sudsy solution and rinse.
3. If it's of a size to dunk the leaves, moisten soil first to prevent fallout.
4. Repeat weekly, three times at least.

SOAPY WATER SOLUTION: One tablespoon of soap powder (don't use detergents) dissolved in a quart of tepid water will make a spray or dunk solution. Apply rubbing alcohol with a cotton swab on mealy bugs; use an old toothbrush dipped in suds to remove scale.

MEALY BUG: Fuzzy grey-white ovals, large enough to be seen; they hide in joints, against stems, sucking juices. Look for leaf-yellowing; deforming of plant.

APHIDS: Wingless insects, green, brown, black, red; suckers on leaves, stems and buds. Look for leaf curl, yellowing, and stickiness which attracts black mold.

SPIDER MITES: Microscopic red or green suckers which make fine webs in joints, on undersides of leaves. Look for leaf curl, buds which don't open and yellow spots.

SCALE: A crawler which grows a brown shell, usually on leaf vein or on main stem; various sizes to one-eighth inch. Look for stickiness on floor near plant.

THRIPS: These are chewers, will strip a leaf to a skeleton if left alone without treatment. Look for signs of small brown or white marks on leaves, flowers.

FUNGUS GNATS: Flying, crawling on top of soil, these lay eggs of maggots in roots. Household-spray gnats; drown eggs in solution of 1 tbsp. bleach to a gallon of water added to the soil.

WHITE FLY: Pinhead-size suckers which flit in clouds when disturbed; they leave a sticky "honeydew" which attracts fungi, molds. Look for leaves yellowing and dropping.

INSECTS AND PESTS

Q *Will ladybugs really eat mealy on a house plant?*

A Hungry ladybugs can lick their weight in mealies, aphids. Start with one or two brought in from the garden and place on the infested plant. When the plant is clean, let the ladybugs fly away home.

Q *What will work on little wrigglers in the soil?*

A Mix a tablespoon of household bleach into a gallon of water; let it stand for an hour, then soak the pot in the solution.

Q *How will I keep earthworms from moving into my pots when I sink them into the soil in summer?*

A Dig the hole for the pot, add a layer of pebbles in the bottom and one of newspaper on that. The pebbles slow down roots which might grow into the soil. The paper keeps out worms.

Q *What would cause cactus rot? I only water once a month in summer.*

A Look with a magnifying glass at the base of the cactus. Brown mites will feed there, making it easy for rot to start. Try a miticide like Kelthane; or make a cutting and reroot, using the solution to be sure trouble isn't repeated.

Q *How can I get rid of algae in a pebble tray?*

A Try a small amount of household bleach each time you change the water in the tray. Be sure the water level doesn't touch the pot's bottom.

Q *I got rid of some tiny worms in the soil of my Ficus benjamina with a solution of household bleach and water. But now, all the new leaves are dropping off. Is it going to die?*

A If your *Ficus* is putting out new leaves it's not going to die. What has happened is that the young roots may have been attacked by the worms, or maggots, and the root system can't support the new leaves. Cut back your *Ficus,* top and sides, to thin out the plant. This will give it time to recover and get bushy again.

Q *Someone told me cigarette tobacco will kill bugs in the soil. Is this true?*

A The nicotine in tobacco is commonly used to get rid of soil invaders. Don't spread the leaves on top of the soil—that's messy; rather, make a "tea" by soaking the tobacco in water overnight. One application should do the job.

Q *My plants developed aphids while I was away for a month and I had to throw them out. Will the pebbles on the trays underneath carry these insects to new plants?*

A It is possible. I suggest that you boil all the pebbles in a big kettle before using again. Also, sterilize the pebble trays with a strong solution of household bleach.

Q *Why do the black aphids on my ivy still cling to the leaves after I've dunked the plant in soapy water?*

A They are tough little buggers, and you may have to dunk at least twice again. If the leaves are particularly infested, cut off the tips of the branches where they grow and destroy them. Even the pressure of hosing does not remove the most tenacious ones.

Index

INDEX

INDEX

ABOUT THE AUTHOR

Maggie Baylis has been practicing plant parenthood for some 25 years. In college she studied architecture, later worked in advertising, and for four years was assistant art director for *Sunset Magazine.* Then in 1951, after her marriage to the late Douglas Baylis, nationally known landscape architect, she found her true niche in life. For twenty years she worked closely with her husband as draftsman, delineator and house plant tender, as well as collaborating with him on articles and as consultants for the nation's leading home and garden publications.

In 1973, Maggie Baylis' first book, *House Plants for the Purple Thumb,* was published, and with little fanfare or publicity became a nationwide best seller. Within two years a half-million copies were sold in both hardcover and paperback editions in North America. During 1975-76 foreign editions will be published in England, Australia and the Netherlands.

Between her numerous television, radio and lecture appearances, Maggie Baylis lives quietly in her unorthodox, plant-filled studio/home on San Francisco's Telegraph Hill, writing and working as consultant.